NOW
THE TIME!

ALSO BY GEORGE BENDALL

Holy Days and Holidays
Blessed Occasions for Heart and Mind

Collected Essays of George Bendall
Includes "Ernest Holmes Remembered"

GEORGE BENDALL, EDITOR

The Holmes Papers:
Talks and Writings of Ernest Holmes

Volume 1 *The Philosophy of Ernest Holmes*
Volume 2 *The Anatomy of Healing Prayer*
Volume 3 *Ideas of Power*

NOW

THE TIME!

Coming Home to Healing Prayer

GEORGE BENDALL, L.H.D.

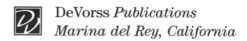

DeVorss *Publications*
Marina del Rey, California

© 2000 Ann Bendall

ISBN: 0-87516-733-0
Library of Congress Catalog Card Number: 00-130313

DEVORSS & COMPANY, Publishers
BOX 550
MARINA DEL REY CA 90294-0550

Printed in the United States of America

CONTENTS

FOREWORD

GEORGE BENDALL (1919–1992) was a graduate from the distinguished ranks of a few hundred very bright young people exempted by President Franklin Roosevelt from military service in World War II for their unique value to the home front—junior "brain-trusters," whose various expertise (George's was engineering) was too valuable to consign to the fortunes of the battlefield. He then joined the ranks of Ernest Holmes' own bright young (and not-so-young) people in the even more fundamental cause of Religious Science and its philosophy, the Science of Mind, of which Holmes was founder and formulator.*

So bright did Holmes find his new minister that, upon the death of Holmes' wife, he moved him into the now very empty Holmes mansion as his aide-de-camp, church-headquarters liaison, and companion in the long night hours devoted to discussion and spiritual prayer treatment. Dr. Bendall has given us an absorbing account of those years in his memoir, "Ernest Holmes Remembered."†

After Holmes' death, Dr. Bendall assumed the pastorate of several Religious Science churches. Increasingly, however, he saw his mission as one of promoting the personal record and memory of his mentor as well as his teachings. To

---

* For a fuller account of Dr. Bendall, see *Collected Essays of George Bendall,* pp. 1–7. The classic statement of the Science of Mind is to be found in Ernest Holmes' *The Science of Mind.*
† *Collected Essays of George Bendall,* pp.97–132.

accomplish this, he instituted a traveling lectureship, available to Religious Science churches everywhere. Further, he personally financed the publication of three volumes of talks by Dr. Holmes—*The Holmes Papers* series, a major document of the Religious Science movement.

Dr. Bendall saw a new opportunity of doing more for Religious Science when he was called upon to serve as interim pastor of the prestigious Founder's Church of Religious Science in Los Angeles upon the death of its first pastor, Dr. William Hornaday. Sadly, however, his time in this post was brief, and he passed away after only seven months in it.

Now the Time! was Dr. Bendall's first book, and it embodies his hands-on, *take-charge* approach of active mental treatment, or metaphysical prayer. As Dr. Holmes had taught for more than 40 years, echoing the English metaphysician Thomas Troward: the individual is *a center of divine operation,* carrying the creative process forward in his or her own right. Dr. Bendall would say that our good does not "happen" to us—*ever.* We *make* it happen—*always.*

In *Now the Time!* George Bendall does what the Science of Mind is all about: he brings the divine meaning of life *down to earth* by showing us how to use true, effective, healing prayer (or *treatment* or any other word you prefer) to adjust our affairs and make things right— again or for the first time. He therefore gets us to work on our lives *here and now* by removing from them everything we don't want. The truly *scientific* way in which this is done he calls *the Law of Eradication.* Its special technique he describes as *Reversing the Reverser.*

The joy of it is, *it works.*

Nor is that all. With the *clearing out* comes the *building in*—of the right things, the whole things; the divine things. And for this we are shown an even greater law than that of eradication: *the Law of Mind in Action*—and how it works.

Some may think all this has a familiar ring, but it doesn't quite the way George Bendall tells it. The book has a unique way of making sense—of instructing, encouraging. It especially seems to have in view the reader who is really, *and now seriously,* trying to change his or her life by staying with prayer—*but in the new way shown here.*

Therefore in these pages Dr. Bendall is *persistent:* because he knows that *we too* are persistent —persistent in putting up with our problems and with the thought-habits that beget and sustain them. But it need not be so. This book can work with you—and you with it—to a very different end.

Naturally, it cannot do the job *for you,* any more than Dr. Bendall himself could if you were counseling with him. But the tools and the method are here; and your steady, patient use of them is guaranteed—yes, *guaranteed*—to work. Perhaps because this is the distillation of those long nights with Ernest Holmes—nights in which two *activists* talked, analyzed, and prayed—*successfully*—into the light of a new day.

ANN BENDALL, Dr. Bendall's wife, has shared intimately in his ministry, and since his passing she has kept his work alive. She has sustained the precious legacy of the three-volume *Holmes Papers* series, including financing and overseeing the corrected, paperback edition of Vol. 1, *The Philosophy of Ernest Holmes*. She has also seen into publication a gathering of Dr. Bendall's talks, including the priceless and historically important memoir of Ernest Holmes in *Collected Essays of George Bendall,* and the later, delightful celebration titled *Holy Days and Holidays.* Her culminating ambition has long been to bring back this her husband's first and most popular book.

CHAPTER 1

HOW DOES SCIENCE ANSWER
WHY? HOW DO *YOU?*

*Those who speak of the incompatibility of
science and religion either make science say
that which it never said or make religion
teach that which it never taught.*

—Pope Pius XI

IN A WORLD still struggling to learn the complex mechanics of survival, peace, and love, science pushes forward at an ever-faster rate. Humanity, meanwhile, has moved across the face of the Earth with ever-increasing force and power, reshaping the physical world to suit its own ends. In the early dawn of humankind, it was crude muscle-power that counted for most. Today, the feeblest muscle could push a button, and millions would be demolished in a nuclear holocaust.

Primitive people had to use muscle to build their houses, kill animals for food, and perform the myriad daily duties that made survival possible. Later, they discovered how to harness animals, water, steam, electric power. Today, we confront nuclear power. And just as the first human must have looked up to the stars and asked the universal question "*Why?*" so we need to do the same thing.

We have for some time now been in the Space Age. Science is asking ever bigger questions and finding more and more of the answers. We reach for the stars—and beyond—stretching our inquiring hands outwards in an endless and untiring search for the unknown.

THE POWER OF MIND

Yet in the midst of all these strivings, there has existed an ever-present inner Power that has moved us steadily along to still higher quests and goals. This Power we refer to as the power of Mind. Our part has been the continuous asking of the universal question "*Why?*" As though by way of self-reply, we have been finding answers we never realized existed.

If the first human had not asked "*Why?*" to all that surrounded him or her, there might never have arisen the idea of a Creator. It is our very nature to wonder and question and seek; and it was also this side of us that brought about the struggles, conflicts, ambitions, and beliefs that were the cause, at many times throughout history, of the great political and religious wars. As each found an answer, each was willing to fight to the bitter end for it.

SOMETHING SURROUNDS US

Now we proceed further into the Space Age, at the turn of a new century and millennium, *still* looking out across the vast expanse of the Universe and *still* wanting to know "*Why?*"—*still* the universal question. We are aware that there is a "reason" behind what surrounds us. We are aware of a cause, a way, a form, a logical process and method that we can—through study—understand.

The more we become aware of the reality that there is a reason, rhythm, and cause for our being, the more we realize that some Power greater than ourselves encompasses all. *There Is a Power That Holds Us Together and Surrounds Us Like a "Gluing" Force.* Call it atomic power, call it Mathematical Principle, Divine Mind, Infinite Intelligence. Call it *X;* call it what you will. In this book we will use the word *God,* but also a variety of names—because it's not the name that is important; it's the *reality*—and whether it *works.*

3

THIS POWER CAN BE USED

Spiritual Mind power, like the more physical "man" power, can be used in *everyday* living in the performance of simple or complex tasks, such as shouldering responsibility, accepting one's self, conquering egocentricity, rising above fear, overcoming doubt, and dispelling worry.

This inner strength, which is as much a part of us as the natural ability to question and seek and know, works through us and can bring confidence and security to our every action.

Our inner and outer necessities, real or imagined, have made us scientists! We have reached into the Earth and through the knowledge of science built a new world.

First the Universe made humanity, then humanity began trying to remake the Universe, cutting trees, making them into lumber, reshaping and using the results for building of shelters and finally beautiful modern buildings using steel and other contemporary materials. We have even reached out to the planets and contemplated populating them.

But more importantly: *We Can Reach Within and Build Inner Structures of Happiness and Creative Fulfillment That Could Never Be Achieved Otherwise.*

WHAT WE'RE DOING HERE

In *Now the Time!* we are therefore interested in scientifically exploring the processes of the mind and learning through the *Law of Eradication* (which we'll explain) to shear the walls of hate, fear, unhappiness, and lack of love.

But what do we mean by *scientifically*? A mere word?

A series of letters connected in order to relabel the old formulas of the past into up-to-date language? No!

Scientifically means the use of what knowledge we have and can *prove*. From the viewpoint of science, *life* is a label for certain recognized ways of reacting. Life can persist only as long as the organism can "trade" with the environment. If we make an *overtrade*, in something like the relationship between carbon dioxide and oxygen, death follows.

Therefore, to achieve an effective adjustment to our total environment is to establish a harmonious relationship with the internal, physical, external, and spiritual. This adjustment is obtained by using the *scientific* way—not the superstitious way.

Since its earliest days, the human race has been concerned with the control of all the processes of nature. At first they were awkwardly "explained" by the use of magic and so-called supernatural dogmas and doctrines. Today we demand *scientific* answers.

AS IT *IS*—NOT AS WE *WISH*

When we attempt to understand what is around us, we do it in one of two ways: either we fashion our understanding of the Universe in the image of our own dreams, or we shape our dreams to fit reality. This latter way is what we mean by the scientific way: *shaping our dreams to fit reality.*

By this method we seek and find the truth, and we use it *as it works*—not the way we *wish* it to work. A car runs only when fuel is put into the tank; if we use water, it won't run.

So works the Universe. If we want a result, we have a much better chance of getting it by going about it scientifically. *Scientifically* means "*as it is*": the use of systematic knowledge—sensibly. A scientist, therefore, is one who uses a universal principle drawn from the laws of nature.

Once a principle is discovered and the laws governing it are confirmed, the scientist maintains an *absolute faith* in that principle. The scientist's *understanding* of it may not be complete; but he or she will work on the principle *as if* it were understood completely, because it has proven itself through use in experimentation.

HOW MUCH *DO* WE HAVE TO UNDERSTAND?

Though we may not understand the basic principles of electricity, we can still use it to light a lamp. In the same way, we don't have to understand the "basic principles of God" to light a candle in the dimness of our knowledge and use what we do know works.

As the scientist can and does maintain an absolute faith in the laws of electricity without necessarily knowing exactly how they function, we can have absolute faith in proven God-principles.

There Are Proven God-Principles! This book is about them—and about taking the mystery out of God.

"Two and two equal four." We don't have to know *why*—only that they do. The reasons "why" could fill a book twice this length if we wanted to go into detail—*but why bother?* All that we need to know is that the principle works: 2 + 2 = 4!

WE USE WHAT WE'VE GOT

This is not to say that *questioning* is out of place, or that *understanding* is undesirable or useless. It is simply to say that while it is fine to ask "*Why?*" lack of the answer should not keep us from using whatever knowledge or understanding we *do* have, however little.

Though the scientist might be concerned with the universal question "*Why?*" he or she does not have to fully understand in order to make a truth work. Primitive people did not know why they must breathe in order to live. They breathed *automatically*—and lived!

Thomas Edison himself did not understand the science or complete workings of electricity, yet *he used what he had* to develop and power the electric light-bulb. The scientist is not so much concerned with "figuring out" the truth as with *using* it.

AN INTELLIGENT UNIVERSE OF LAW AND ORDER

We are learning through science that intelligence is not limited to humankind, or even to Earth; *Intelligence Is the Very Substance of the Universe!* And there is a law and order to all things.

In ancient times, the answers to the "*Why?*" were interlaced with superstitious fears and explanations. "*The Rain God hasn't given us rain because we didn't slaughter enough sheep in his honor!*" The scientific mind within all of us began to wonder how the killing of sheep could bring rain.

The longer we humans explored, the more we found, and the more we saw of the rhythm and intelligent order of things.

The world-famous physicist and author James Jeans explained that "The Universe shows evidence of a designing power that has something in common with our own individual mind."

Nobel-Prize-winning physicist Robert Millikan flatly stated that "God is a God who rules through law, not whim."

The equally world-famous astronomer Arthur Eddington went further in asserting that "Prayer influences the course of physical phenomena when directed to these centers."

A GOD OF SCIENCE AND A SCIENCE OF GOD

Science, so far from disproving these grand truths about the Universe, is in fact *proving* them, and in terms that the questioning mind can accept—without feeling it is being preached to, or that its intelligence is being insulted.

We do not need the superstitious blind faith of the Dark Ages. This is the "postmodern" age, in which the things that are accepted are things *known* and *expected to work* in mathematical order, according to scientific principle. *This Should Prove to Be True of God as Well!*

When we speak of God, we are not speaking of some "being" that we turn to in the desperation of need and whom we beg for help. We are talking about nothing less than a "mathematical" Force that works automatically when we tune into It (not that this is by any means all that there is to God).

When you turn a radio on, you tune in to the radio waves, which are already everywhere about, available for use. When we pray, we tune in to a genuine God-Power that is similarly *already there,* available for us to use. *But It's Up to Us to "Tune In"!*

CAN WE "USE" GOD?

Atomic energy was everywhere about (and within) us before we discovered how to use it in (at first) destructive ways in the 1940s. Scientists did not make or create atomic power—they discovered what was already there. How to use it and how to control it was their task.

God Is There, Functioning Right Now, Working and Shaping Automatically All Things within the Universe into the Rhythm and Perfect Form That the God-Force Created in the First Place. It Is When We Resist the God-Force that We Get into Trouble.

As we realize that there is an intimate relationship between ourselves and God and begin working in the same direction with the rhythm of the Universe, the God-Force manifests in our everyday life and satisfies our inner hunger.

As we realize that we are in essence one with everything and know that in our creative meditation or true prayer great mountains can be removed automatically, we become convinced that *It Is <u>within Ourselves</u> to Use the Power of Mind—Intelligence—to Create for Us What We Need and Desire.*

As "Science knows nothing of opinion, but recognizes a government of law whose principles are universal" (Ernest Holmes), we shall not—*could not*—ask for anything more. Ernest Holmes further says, in his *The Science*

9

of Mind: "Revelation must keep faith with reason, and religion with law."

BUT THE LAW IS ALSO *PERSONAL*

It was Jesus who added to the Law of Moses the warmth of love and the knowledge that a divine Presence is within the Universe and can, to each one of us, be warm and personal.

Another Nobel-Prize-winner in physics, Arthur Compton, believed that science had discovered nothing to contradict the idea that there is a divine Presence and a Universal Mind intimately personal to each one of us. And the great geneticist and biochemist John Haldane claimed that the only creative thing that science has discovered is *Mind*—that *The Laws of the Universe Are Intelligence Acting as Law.*

A REVOLUTION IN RELIGION

When Phineas Parkhurst Quimby (1802–1866) started a revival of spiritual mind healing about 150 years ago, a major revolution in religion took place, resulting in the formation of such metaphysical religious groups as Christian Science, Unity, Divine Science, Home of Truth, Church of the Truth, and Religious Science. Of course there were, and continue to be, many others.

There is one thing that all of these groups have in common with each other: the conviction that there is something within us that can heal through the action of prayer.

A major premise of Quimby's spiritual philosophy is

that what one person can do (he especially had Jesus in mind), another can do, *provided there is present the same degree of belief, feeling, and understanding.*

HEALING IS <u>NORMAL</u>

Healing for health and perfection is normal. Jesus not only taught—he was a successful healer; and his students went out and "did likewise." In fact, all great religious leaders have taught that it is possible for anyone to use the powers that they discovered *provided one "tunes in."*

THE LAW OF ERADICATION

For example, Jesus learned the *Law of Eradication* (so will you, in these pages) and had the ability to use it for the healing of others. When he said to the palsied man, "Arise and walk!" he was demonstrating his ability to *Ignore the Imperfect and See Only the Perfect.*

He realized that the only thing that causes imperfection is the failure of the individual to erase the conflicts in their conscious awareness. In other words, they have not discovered how to use the *Law of Eradication* to drop from their world the things they do not wish to experience.

Therefore, disease, imperfection, and disharmony are not a matter of morals or physical disrepair, but rather *a matter of our own mind.* There is a *right* way of thinking, then acting and reacting, in order to function properly and to have all parts working in perfect synchronization and rhythm. *But This Demands the Eradication of Negative Ideas and Inner Conflicts.*

"SIN NO MORE"

The dictionary defines *Holy* (which is how we refer to God) as *wholeness,* or *completeness.* If we are "in the image of God," we must be *essentially* whole. To be "God-like" is to be holy, or *whole.* To be whole, one must, like those Jesus healed, *"arise and walk."*

As we attune ourselves to *what is*—God—we "arise and walk"; we begin to enter the Kingdom of Heaven! We achieve the state of being that is truly "holy." As Ernest Holmes says, *"There Is No Sin but a Mistake, and No Punishment but an Inevitable Consequence."*

We are concerned in *Now the Time!* to show a *method of attuning ourselves to perfection.* Once we can accept that *all* is wholeness, rather than *partial* wholeness—which is really nothing but a mental resistance to the normal rhythm of the Universe—then our mistakes/conflicts *will* be released, and our consequences will not be "punishments." This is what it is to "sin no more."

THE SCIENTIFIC LAW OF MIND

The scientific assumption is that nothing moves but Intelligence. This is what Eddington meant when he said, "We can think of all the laws of nature as though they were intelligence acting as law." Or as Jeans put it: "We can think of it as an infinite Thinker."

While the thought may be spontaneous, the way it works and what happens constitute a *mathematical and mechanical reaction* to the "cause" that our thought is.

A law is in action here—*the Law of Mind.* It indeed works automatically, with scientific logic and mathematical certainty—in other words, *intelligently.*

It responds to thoughts. Our thoughts drop like seeds into its "pool of energy" and create a disturbance—reaction—and the effect is the automatic result.

OUR THOUGHTS ARE THE "MOVER"

Pythagoras was pointing this out when he said, "All is motion and numbers; but there is a mover." *Our Thought—the Mover—Automatically Causes a Reaction in the Creative Power, Which Works Intelligently and with Mathematical Precision*—the precision, you might say, of numbers. Even music, one of our most emotional expressions, can be reduced to numbers. In fact, rhythm and order are *precise*—and our thoughts yield results in just the same way.

A TECHNIQUE WE CAN USE

Our whole technique and practice, therefore, is based on the premise that *Mind in Action Works as Law.* Whenever we create a *mental* state relative to anything and *identify* with that mental state, it tends to become manifested in our experience. What we project mentally becomes our reality. And if we make affirmative *statements* to this effect—i. e. put it into affirmative prayer—the thing projected will likely emerge even sooner in our experience.

In *Now the Time!* we are dealing with what we call the *Law of Eradication. The Law of Eradication Is the Art of Dropping from Our Thoughts What We Do Not Wish to Experience.* In prayer, we drop the thoughts that are

13

responsible for the problem or disorder that is afflicting us at the moment.

THINK WHAT YOU LIKE!

We can think anything we want to think, and that thought will become our reality. Think negatively, and we will experience negative results. Think affirmatively, and automatically "good" will result. This is what Jesus meant when he said, "It is done unto you as you believe." Since we are the only ones who can think ourselves into a difficulty, we are the only ones who can *unthink* our way out of it. "It all arises out of a thought, and a thought can melt it away," said Ralph Waldo Emerson.

WORDS OF POWER

"Ye shall know the truth and the truth shall set ye free," stated Jesus. Two thousand years ago, this man awakened the world to the ability, in all of us, to demonstrate through Mind the things that we wish to experience.

When he said, "The words that I speak are Spirit and Life," he meant that *because of his understanding of the healing principles of God,* he had the power to speak his words *and they would automatically get results.* His words had the power of Spirit and Life because *He Knew How to Project Them Effectively into the Creative Power of Mind,* which always responded to them.

Further, he taught that what *he* could do, *we* too could do. When he said, "The words that I speak are Spirit and Life," he was saying, for all of us, that *"The*

Word That We Speak" Is Whatever We Believe. And as we "speak" it, it is "done unto us."

HOW HE DID IT

Jesus had no doubt that what he said would become visible and result in exactly what he had implied it would become in his thinking/conviction. "Thy servant is healed!" "Water to wine!" "Lazarus, come forth!" "Take up thy bed and walk!"

Jesus did not ask; he did not *plead;* he did not *beg.* He simply stated what he wanted, *expecting to get it*—not with hopes or dreams, but just because *He Knew That What He Wanted Was Already There, Ready for Him to Have but for the "Tuning in" and Making Known His Desires.*

He wasn't talking in terms of something miraculous; he was stating that he expected a certain thing to happen or take place or appear—*and it did!*

HE HAD IT *HIS* WAY

He Was Specific! He knew that, once "tuned in" to his Father—or, if you prefer, the God-Power—he could get exactly what he said he wanted. His word was the Cause; what he received as a result of his word was the Effect (which is *automatic*).

There is a reason for everything that takes place: a scientific, "mathematical" reason. Our word is the *cause* or *action* or *impression.* That cause automatically produces its effect the moment our word is spoken with the same conviction and faith with which Jesus spoke his word into the All-Knowing Universal Mathematical Principle, which is All-Intelligence and what we call *God*.

Simply put, *There Is No Difference Whatever between the Thought and the Form It Takes!*

WHAT IS OUR *REAL* THOUGHT?

Thoughts are ideas that project themselves into reality. If we *say* we are healed, but believe deep down inside that we are *not* (this being our real thought/conviction), *we will not be healed!* It is not mouthing words that works; it is knowing that what we say is true and that *it will work. The Cause Is in the Conviction.*

When we say *Now the Time!* we are saying, "Let's KNOW it *Now!*" Just as Jesus was specific when he made a demonstration or healing, *we* must be specific. We must KNOW that our word is Law in action. We must KNOW that as we speak (think) our word (cause), we get the demonstration (effect).

NOTHING PHONY, MAGICAL, OR TRICKY

We are not dealing with the supernatural. We are dealing with the natural laws of God that created the Universe and that hold it in order and form. We are not suggesting magical statements. We are not proposing anything that is trick or miracle. The only "wand" we will ever wave is compliance with the laws of nature working mathematically.

A religion or concept small enough to be super-easily understood wouldn't be large enough for our needs. The way toward understanding or knowing the answer to the universal question "*Why?*" is *not* all that easy, in the sense that it doesn't come without study, practice, and hard work. Yes, it requires time and patience.

The difference between manifesting a visible demonstration out of our conviction/word and not manifesting it is the difference between just *mouthing* our desire and KNOWING it. To learn how to pray in the *Now!* we must know and understand the "secret": *Meaning What We Say and Saying What We Mean.*

IT'S UP TO US

God gave us intelligence—and freedom to use it in our own way. This intelligence is one with the Universal Intelligence and functions in the same precise, mathematical manner. As the first human looked up at the heavens and asked "*Why?*"so we must turn *inwards* and find our answer there—by learning how to speak our word—and learning that it is done to us just as we deeply believe.

We must go inward, into the mind itself, and tune it in to the All-Powerful Intelligence that is flowing through us. We must learn to *believe* our word, and then *Speak Only What We Believe and Know*—for this is *Now the Time!*

CHAPTER 2

WHAT ARE YOU *KNOWING* ABOUT YOURSELF?

What we know, we have no opinion of.

—Phineas Parkhurst Quimby

LITTLE PEGGY was praying at her bedside. As she knelt there, clasping her hands tightly together, she said, "Please, God, help Daddy in his business, and Aunt Julie to get her television set, and my little dog Fluffy to be happy all the time. But most of all, help Mommy to get well!" She paused and added an extra special something: "And please, God, take care of *yourself;* 'cause if anything ever happened to *you,* we'd all be in an *awful* mess!"

It would seem that God answered that last part, because He's still around and in business.

WHAT PEGGY *KNEW*

"*God created the heavens and the Earth . . .*" and all things in the Universe. This Creative Power and Intelligence that we call God is here all around us, "closer than hands and feet," to be used in everyday living. And as Peggy prayed, so are *we* able to pray and use this God-Power to change our lives.

The extraordinary—and in some ways *ironic*—thing about this is that **We Are Using This God-Power All the Time in Our Everyday Thinking, Acting, and Speaking.** Yes, the very same processes that are active when we *think* are the ones that are used in praying and getting demonstrations (= answers to prayers).

Peggy KNEW that her Daddy's business would be helped, that Aunt Julie would get her television set, and that her dog Fluffy would be made happy. She KNEW that her mother would be made well and that God would take care of Himself! She KNEW, because she had faith in

God and in the effectiveness of her prayers. She KNEW
with a child-like faith.

LET YOUR FAITH BE *KNOWING*

The key is to KNOW. As a little child prays with what scientists might call "blind faith," KNOWING that the
prayer will be answered, so must everyone who wants the
answer to their prayers KNOW that what they say *will*
happen.

Science says: faith is a mental attitude so inwardly
impressed that the mind can no longer deny it. Better
still: *Faith Is an Ironclad Belief in the Presence of an
Invisible Law That Directly and Specifically Responds
to Us.* This is what Jesus meant when he said, "as you believe . . . "

Faith originally had a religious sense and still has
emotional overtones. But in this book we are going to
banish the word *blind* from *blind faith* and show how to
replace the overused *believe* with *KNOW.*

Just as science employs universal principles, faith can
be seen as the scientific use of still another universal principle—the Law of Mind. Note too that as the scientist
discovers the laws governing the physical Universe, he or
she must maintain an absolute "faith" in these discoveries
in order to be able to use them in practical ways. In fact,
the very business of discovering new laws is based on an
implicit *faith* in the "old" laws!

TO BE A CHILD AGAIN

For *our* needs, we must have the "child-like" KNOWING of little Peggy.

Children see each new day as a wonderful adventure, living in a fantasy-world of their own making. They *believe* in their fantasies; they *believe* in Peter Pan, elves, magic, Santa Claus. They *believe* that when a tooth is put under their pillow at night, the Tooth Fairy will leave some money in its place for them to find in the morning. In this seemingly child-like awareness, *They Are Doing What We Must Learn to Do All Over Again, if We Wish to Pray Effectively.*

Children expect to live a new adventure when they awake to a new day. They inhabit a world of belief—*as the child believes, so it is*—but then they grow up, and each belief is shattered by cruel "reality." Too soon there begins the struggle for survival in the world of adulthood.

If at that time, however, *our beliefs become visions of success* in the home, business, and life; if we believe—and work hard enough to make our dreams come true—we *do* become what we had "dreamed" we would.

NOT SOMETHING FOR NOTHING

It requires hard work and a lot of faith to sustain ourselves through "dry spells." If that faith is not there—that is, if we don't KNOW that we'll be successful—we allow defeat after defeat to discourage us until finally we give up. But if, *like a child*, we KNOW we are going to be successful, nothing in the world can stop us, and we will continue until we get what we desire. We will push forward *regard-*

less of what it takes—because we *believe in* our dreams.
Because we have faith.
Because we KNOW that we will be successful.
And so we become.

Because the "faith" has kept us going, striving, working for that goal which we KNOW will be the automatic result of our efforts. We *believe in* our dreams, and they come true.

DON'T LOSE YOUR FAITH BY THE "WISHING WELL"!

It is not enough just to *wish*. *We Follow Up Our Wishes with Effort.* We learn that through faith we are able to mentally, emotionally, and spiritually sustain ourselves until the "dream" becomes the reality.

We all, at some time or another, meet a severe test of faith—and pass it. We either continue to live creatively—or we destroy ourselves day by day, until we become a fatality of our inability to have faith in the *Now!*

THE *REAL* NATURE OF "OLD AGE"

This lack of faith is what we call *old age*—for *Old Age Is Nothing but the Waning of Faith in Life.* Those who have lost faith have nothing to live for; they do not believe in themselves, those around them, their present, or their future.

We have all seen older people; they seem to come in two major types: those waiting for death to take them and those so busy living that they don't have time to think of death—*or even of old age!* The ones awaiting death sit around already half dead, looking across the void at a world that they now feel they are not a part of.

They *look* old.

"The world's gone to hell," they often say.

They find everything an effort—even breathing—and they sometimes go so far as to "wish" themselves into the grave.

THE "OTHER" PEOPLE

The *other* people are *alive!* They don't know what old age is. And if it finally does overtake them, slowing them down—well, it's just "inconvenient."

They are like John Quincy Adams. When a very old man, the ex-president was stopped on the streets of Boston by a friend who hadn't seen him for a long time. Shaking his trembling hand, the man inquired anxiously, "And how is John Quincy Adams these days?"

The ex-president smiled warmly, his face lined with wrinkles, his eyes sparkling.

> *I am fine, thank you; but the house in which John Quincy Adams lives at present is becoming a little run down. The foundations are beginning to shake as if the very earth were about to swallow it up. Time has weakened the structure until it is nearly about to crumble to dust. The roof is fairly well worn through. The walls are cracked and already beginning to disintegrate, and they shake and vibrate at the slightest breeze. The old place is becoming just about uninhabitable, and I think that John Quincy Adams will*

*be moving out very soon. But he himself is quite
well; quite well indeed!*

Old age is only a thing of the mind. *It Is a Mental
Resistance against the Very Laws of Nature.* The laws of
nature are *vitality, growth, excitement, joy, love.* They are
the laws of God.

Old age is that decay which creeps into the conscious
awareness and rots there, making useless persons out of
people who should, *through their very experience of living
in the past,* be all the more vitalized and eager to love,
enjoy, grow, and project more creatively and effectively.

A YOUTH IN HIS SEVENTIES

Though in his seventies, Howard acted as though he were
closer to twenty. *He enjoyed living!* To see him in a group,
you would be surprised to discover how old he really was,
for in the expression of his lined face, the light in his eager
eyes, the way his voice would excitedly flow and half sing,
the springing swing of his walk, he was more like a teenager—because he was enjoying every moment he lived as if
it were his last . . . or perhaps his first.

He joined in and became an important part of the
world around him. He belonged to social clubs, was president of a thriving business, active in political elections,
organizer of drives, dinners, benefit parties, and shows to
collect money and clothes for the poor.

He helped young people "find" themselves and
encouraged them to perform creatively for those around
them.

Once acquainted with Howard, however, they made the

startling discovery that he had been living on the edge of death for over thirty years!

Medical science had said he had only six months to live—*when he was still in his thirties!*

Here was a man who, because of the inner joy of living, displayed behavior that belied his "old age" by giving him that youthful zest of living which not even every young person always displays.

HER FAITH WAS IN DEFEAT

Tyrone Edwards must have known persons like Howard and John Quincy Adams, for he said, "Some men are born old, and some never seem so. If we keep well and cheerful, we are always young, and at last die in youth, even when years would count us old."

Some people are too busy *living* and *creating* to be bothered with old age. Others are old before their time, because they have allowed themselves to become discouraged. They are defeated people who have arrived at their discouragement through loss of faith not only in themselves but in others—even in life itself.

Clara, a woman in her mid-forties, believed she had nothing to live for. Her husband had left her for another woman; the son she had raised was not independent. She felt that there was nothing left of her world.

When her husband returned, begging for forgiveness, she refused to take him back. All her life she had lived religiously and faithfully, but she could not swallow her false pride. The church she belonged to proscribed smoking and drinking—outlets to which she now turned, as an escape from the unpleasant "reality" her life had become.

Not only did she smoke and drink, but she finally sought companionship in cocktail lounges, private clubs, and expensive nightclubs. She rejected everything that had been a part of her happiness with her husband; she dropped her church social-work activity; and the accustomed love she had given to those around her was now turning into hate.

In other words, the love she had shared with her husband was now ruining both their lives—even though (and perhaps especially because) it was still felt secretly by each. Neither would give in now, and the separation became permanent.

When her ex-husband died, she quickly dropped even further away from the life she had lived. She left the country and went around the world. When she returned, she claimed she had a heart ailment that gave her only a short time to live. Sure enough, she soon died.

It was later discovered by her relatives that *there had been nothing really wrong with her heart*. In fact, she had been in good health with a chance for a wonderfully creative and enjoyable life, including helping others, as she had done in the past.

But with the loss of her husband, she had given up hope—and faith in the future. From that moment, she stopped living and instead began dying bit by bit—because she had lost interest in life. *She Had Lost Faith in Others and Faith in Herself and—Finally—Faith in Living.*

DRIED UP AND BLOWING AWAY

"There is no great future for any people whose faith has burned out or congealed," the American Quaker Rufus M. Jones once pointed out. People who give up, be they young or old, are the only ones that have taken on "old age." They have lost the very qualities that are so apparent in a little child: *joy, vivacity, radiance, innocence, excitement, wonder.* They have lost the very qualities that make living such a wonderful thing.

They have lost the sense of wonder, the ability to fantasize and imagine. They have been bogged down by the "cold realities" of the "hard, uncivilized jungle" everybody says we live in. They have stopped seeing what is *really* around them and have begun seeing what *people say* is around them:

War; financial depression; big business taking over; the world about to be destroyed in a nuclear holocaust; the country going to the dogs; unions not strong enough; unions too strong; the world overpopulated; not enough food; more food than we need; the farmer overproducing. The list is endless and keeps growing.

The "given-up" feel that they have not achieved enough and that they are failures. They have lost the ability to laugh and sing and love and be loved.

That Is Why We Must KNOW with the Same Sense of Wonder As a Child.

NO MAYBES ABOUT IT!

Our mistake is that we believe that *maybe* the miracle could occur. This is not the faith or conviction that we are talking about—the faith or conviction that dissolves all adversity.

Thomas Browne, in *Religio Medici* (1643), said: "To believe only possibilities is not faith, but mere philosophy." It takes more than "mere philosophy" to make dreams come true. And it is not enough to *say* in the face of personal disaster that "This is not the Truth of my being—I know that God will lead me." *We Must Believe It . . . And More.*

It takes understanding, and it takes the *conviction* of what we are believing. It is one thing to say a few beautiful words, but it is quite another to KNOW that this is what we mean—what we are really KNOWING *deep inside.* That is the reason we must take the word *blind* away from *faith* and use the word *KNOW. Having Faith Must Mean KNOWING!*

When we say, "This is not the Truth of my being—I know that God will lead me," we don't mean that there is some thing or being that is pointing a finger and guiding us. We are simply stating:

This [illness, emotional problem, etc.] is not the norm of my existence, and I know that the intelligence within me, which is part of the Universal Intelligence, will guide me through this and any other difficulty. I know I have the ability and the intelligence to see myself through any problem, and I accept this ability as being normal.

BEHIND THE "SAYING"

There is more to just "saying" (even knowing what we are saying) and being scientific about the whole thing. *We Must Learn Our Relationship to the Whole—to the Universe—to What We Call God.*

We must realize these basics and from that beginning use this knowledge to better our lives and heighten the happiness of those around us.

Our whole theory of prayer is based not only on the *belief in God* but on the *availability of God* and the *immediate, automatic response.* We can even go so far as to say, *If We Pray Right, Then God Cannot Help but Respond.*

Phineas Parkhurst Quimby (see p. 10) believed that prayer must be *affirmative,* not negative. In his time he was considered by some a fake and a fraud; but today he is remembered, and his critics are forgotten—*because what he taught proved to be true.*

He taught that what one person could do two thousand years ago, we can do today. He believed that as we progress in our understanding, we more nearly incarnate the "Christ" and achieve the demonstrations that Jesus proved were possible.

MAKING YOUR *YES* THE <u>YES</u> OF POWER

Mary Baker Eddy based her whole Christian Science teaching on this importance of *denying* "error" and *affirming* one's perfection. William R. Parker and Elaine St. Johns, in their book *Prayer Can Change Your Life,* told of the discovery, made in a university-classroom setting, that *prayer therapy is 70 percent more effective when affirma-*

tive. Thus, in a scientific experiment covering months of hard work, Dr. Parker arrived at the same conclusion as Quimby and the illumined religious leaders of all ages.

We have to accept that *Prayer Is Its Own Answer, in the Terms of Its Own Acceptance.* Jesus said, "It is done unto you as you believe." *Nothing Can Come Out of Prayer Unless It Is Put into the Prayer.* Mouthing our words is not putting anything into prayer. It is what we *think, believe,* and KNOW that we put into the prayer.

Without faith—the conviction of our prayer—we get no results. *Faith is the power of prayer.* When we say that *faith is the power of prayer,* we are in effect saying, *Faith Is the Strength of Our Convictions, and That Strength Will Determine the Power (Cause) Our Prayer Will Have and Therefore the Effect It Will Achieve.*

This is the power behind prayer that we are talking about. Without faith, your prayer will not have the necessary power to make it effective. If Jesus had not KNOWN that what he said would come about, *it would not have come about!*

IT'S THE LAW!

As we speak our word with inner conviction—faith (KNOWING)—we will *automatically* get what we have projected into God (i. e. the Law of Mind in Action).

It is like putting an electric plug into the wall socket and then turning on the light switch. We *automatically* get light from the bulb. The electricity was there all the time.

All we have to do is "plug into" the Power of God, which is all around us, ready to be used.

We had complete faith that the light would go on. We KNEW it would go on because of past experience. The electric power was there to be used.

We used it.

A child, seeing a wall socket, might put her finger in it (if she could) and there would follow an "effect" that could be harmful. But when we grow up, we learn what the wall outlet is, *and how to use it.*

In the same way, we can learn how to use faith to "plug into" the God-Power, which is there for us to use.

THE "SECRET" IS SIMPLE

There is one major "law of electricity," and that law works for all electricity. It is the *law* that makes electricity *electricity.*

If the *law* (which rules electricity) changed, then *electricity* would change—and therefore would be something else.

What we define as Mind—be it "human" or "God" Mind—must be of the *same* Mind—*the same Mind principle.* ***If Our Mind Is of the Same Mind As God's, Then We Must Have the Same Mind-Power As God's Mind— and Available to Us.***

In order to pray effectively, we must KNOW effectively. We must KNOW that our prayers will be answered! The "secret" is simple.

THE PRACTICE? WELL . . . *NOT SO EASY*

No, the actual practice is not so easy. And that is why so few people pray effectively. But aren't you glad that this is a *science* and not *abracadabra?*

Who said a *science* was easy, anyway? But the great thing is that, *Though Not "Easy"—It Works!* (By now you know that *abracadabra* and all the other magical-mysterious-&-oh-so-"spiritual" incantations and pleadings and ceremonies and—you name it—*don't* work.)

So we must develop a new mental process. That is what scientists do, isn't it? And we must develop new mental "muscles."

Here is a start:

"I and the Father are One."
I and Spirit are One.
I and Intelligence are One.
I and Right Thinking are One.
I am One with the All-Knowing Intelligence,
Creative Life Principle, Mathematical Force
that is God.

They all say the same thing. *You Have to Mean Them.*

PUT YOUR FINGER ON
THE TRIGGER . . . SQUEEZE!

It is possible to need something, want something, or be determined enough to get something so that when we pray for it, it *will* come about—*because our need will trigger the same process each and every time we want to trigger it.*

33

Everybody has had their prayers answered one time or another. Like little Peggy, speaking to a God that was so real to her that she could almost see Him, some of us were able to heal our parents and friends and loved ones more quickly than any other person could, because we believed with the faith of a little child. We KNEW it would happen. *So it happened.*

But as we grew up, doubts became our way of life. We began asking the universal question "*Why?*" and began getting the scientist's replies. This was normal; for we must and will discover for ourselves the truth about ourselves and what surrounds us—*scientifically.*

The question is normal. But in order to trigger the automatic switch that will power the lightbulb of understanding, *We Must Return to That Child-Like Sense of Wonder and See Things in a "New" Light.* This means using both our mature adult mind and our imaginative processes. *That* is the way to understand more fully the surrounding Universe.

IMAGINATION HOLDS THE KEY

Without imagination, nothing could be created, for it must be thought of in the mind first and then, as an automatic result, projected into reality. And it is in the "child-like" mental attitude that our imagination works the fullest and most creatively.

But this is not to be confused with creating fantasies, for that can be confusion itself! Fantasy is not the purpose of attaining this new mental outlook. Rather, we are opening the channels of our Creative Awareness in order to accept into our lives the good reality that is *already* there, awaiting our recognition—something that our "educated" intellect might cringe at or shrink from.

Our good—the object of our scientific, intelligent, effective prayer—is no fantasy! It's time we saw it rather as the *reality* it has always been. So: ***Now the Time!***

CHAPTER 3

THE SECRET OF EFFECTIVE PRAYER

The first step to knowledge is to know that we are ignorant.

—Cecil

IN ORDER to even begin on the journey of understanding, we must come to the realization that we do not know everything there is to know. We are learning every day. The human race is learning new things all the time—each new moment.

Science is discovering horizons that we never knew existed. Not terribly long ago, a person who thought the world was round was considered mad. Prior to 1945, atomic power was off in the far future. Not many years ago, space flight was considered by the top political minds to be the domain of science-fiction writers. It was only in 1957 that the public was forced to the realization that we weren't in the Nuclear Age any more but had been plunged into the Space Age—and that there was nothing anybody could do about it.

WE MUST BE TEACHABLE

Once we admit that we do not know everything there is to know and we honestly attempt to open our mind to new ideas, we will be ready to start on the journey that leads to the real "Kingdom of Heaven." In this state of mind we will be willing and anxious to learn a new way of thinking and living. *And we will be ready to learn the new attitudes that will lead to effective prayer.*

It is only then that we will truly be an open channel for new understanding and new experiences. It is only then that we will be ready to accept a new, *much* better, way of life.

We must build new habit patterns. We must learn new ways of thinking. For affirmative prayer, we will learn how to speak our words—*and mean them*—and have them become our new reality. "It is done unto you as you believe. . . . All things whatsoever you pray and ask for, *believe that you have [already] received them,* and you *shall* receive them."*

NOW TRY THIS:

> *I accept the intuition of God that reveals to me my heritage. I now clear my thought of all doubts, fears, and questions. I know that Infinite Intelligence guides me into my true expression of life. I know that all "secrets" for my health and peace of mind are now open to me.*

If we say this over and over daily, understanding the truth that it states, and have it become more a part of our way of thinking than any other thought, we will be well on the way to learning the "secret" of Effective Prayer. *Its very simplicity is the "catch."*

It's easy to forget or overlook what we are trying to understand here, and that is why we repeat the same Truth over and over again, in different ways. *It Is the Simple Process of Reshaping and Conditioning Our Thinking along Different, More Effective Lines.*

---

* Mark 11:24 "The difference of the tenses in this passage is remarkable. The speaker [Jesus] bids us first to believe that our desire *has* already been fulfilled, that it is a thing already accomplished, and then its accomplishment *will* follow as a thing in the future. This is nothing else than a concise direction for making use of the creative power of thought. . . ." Thomas Troward, *The Edinburgh Lectures on Mental Science,* p. 31 (DeVorss ed'n).

If prayer that is affirmative is 70 percent more effective than prayer that is not affirmative—*and this has been proven scientifically*—then that is the way to do it. *Every Prayer Must Be a Proclamation of Mind Knowing that It Has the Power to Secure an Effect as a Result of Its Own Words (Cause) and that the Effect Is Spontaneous and Automatic.*

LET'S RECAP FOR JUST A MOMENT

Jesus never departed from logic in anything. He was so simple that many did not want to believe him. His basic teaching was "*I and the Father are one.*" We must have as the first axiom of our own understanding that *Truth Is God, and God Is All-Intelligence* (Mathematical Law and Power working creatively and automatically around and through us). When we pray, we must believe in this greater power than our physical selves. *Without This Assumption as a KNOWN Truth, We Are Wasting Our Time Praying.*

WE GET WHAT WE SEE

When we think disharmoniously, all we see around us is disharmony reflected in people, things, experiences, and actions. For example, almost every one of us has experienced days when we thought that others were talking "behind our back."

We have all known people like John: he thought negatively and disharmoniously not only about his surroundings, home, and business, but about the world itself. He was not only worried about the people who were "talking behind his back"; he was sure his business was going to pot and that everything was horrible, useless, and boring.

John fairly radiated this state of thought. If he saw two people talking by themselves, he thought they were talking about him. If they laughed, they were laughing about him.

We Always See Things as Our Mental Attitude Allows Us to See Them, be they people or conditions. If we believe that conditions are poor and that it is impossible to improve them, then we will do nothing about them. When we find ourselves reacting in this way, it is necessary to *reverse* our outlook. We must turn inward and try to understand *why* we have been holding this mental attitude.

And we must pray.

PLUG IN!

As we "plug in" to the God-Power, knowing we are "one with the Father," we automatically clear our thought of all conflicts, and we have the understanding to see our way out of any difficulty.

But it is up to us. God is not going to come down out of the sky and show us the way. *The Way Is Already; It Is Up to Us to Get with It.*

Plugging in to the God-Power *itself* powers a change in our mental attitude, switching ON our understanding. *It Is Automatic.*

So is God.

So is Mind-Power.

So is Creative Energy.

All of these are the same—they are the Universal Power (or, if you prefer, God); for God is All, in all.

EVERYWHERE—AND NEVER-FAILING

While a young boy was visiting his aunt, she told him she would give him an apple if he would tell her where God is. He quickly replied, saying, "I will give *you* two apples if you will tell me where He is *not!*" God is All, and All is God.

The whole teaching of Jesus was based on the theory that we are surrounded by an intelligent Law that does unto each of us as we believe it will.

OUR PART: THE *PRACTICE*

When the great violinist Niccolò Paganini was asked why it was that he played the guitar before a concert instead of the violin, he replied. "I never rehearse the violin. My practice is in the gymnastics of the guitar, to be sure of my suppleness of finger and touch. My violin then never fails me."

In much the same way, we "practice" prayer and meditation not to "rehearse" God or strengthen His power, but to be sure of our suppleness of understanding and thought. God never fails us.

But we often fail to do our "practice"—to use and understand the powers that are all around us, flowing through us and through everything in the Universe. That is why we must willingly use affirmations—not to convince God of anything, but to teach ourselves a new way of looking at the truth around us—*until This New*

Thought-Process Becomes a Part of Our Way of Life, and our prayers become effective.

NOW LET'S SUMMARIZE

Let us pause here and summarize. Use the following as a checklist. Is there anything in it that you didn't get? . . . overlooked?

1. A prayer is not dependent on any person, place, or thing. It is only dependent upon our own recognition that what we say and believe will become our experience.

2. When we speak with conviction, our word is acted upon AUTOMATICALLY, with mathematical precision, by a Creative Power that is greater than ourselves, but which is around and flowing through us, waiting to be used.

3. We activate this power subconsciously every conscious moment of our lives. The energy of our thoughts, which science has discovered is a measurable energy, is always projecting into our experiences.

4. What we are concerned with is learning to use this power consciously at will, for the exact purpose that we wish to use it for, at the exact moment we wish to use it.

WORRY, WORRY!

We worry, and worry-thoughts project themselves into our experience. Like John, we want to stop worrying but feel it's impossible. However, that's not true! *If We Can Think Ourselves into a Problem, We Can Think Ourselves out of It.* But only *we* can do that thinking; it is up to *ourselves* and nobody else.

When John was told this in conjunction with a statement that a newspaper editor once made—"If I could *worry* a penny into my pocket, I'd *worry* all night"—he realized for the first time that it was *his wrong mental attitude* that made things look dark and grim. It is in confusion that everything looks the darkest.

As John calmed himself and began thinking clearly— *undramatically*—his whole being took on a different rhythm. Once he realized that worry and nervousness would not gain him "one red cent," he discovered it was possible to obtain more than he needed!

No intelligent solution to any problem was ever attained through a sense of confusion, when our thinking processes are not running smoothly. As a machine runs better when cleaned and oiled, so does mind benefit from a "cleansing."

The answer to our problem lies in the subconscious mind, which is our "portion" of the Universal Mind. *When We Are Confused, Worried, and Nervous, We Are Not "Tuned In" to Our Mind Power.* We are then like a broken electric power line, flailing wildly in the air, spurting sparks of power in all directions without any creative effect, but instead with the threat of a terribly destructive result. But as we calm down and "connect" ourselves with the flowing Mind Power, we find the solution to our "problem."

MORE ABOUT *TRUE* PRAYER

We have seen that the Law of Mind works impersonally, like the law of electricity. It is an impersonal Principle, and the more faith we have in this Principle, the more we will be able to use it.

True prayer can therefore be defined as *the Tuning-In Process That Brings Our Conscious Mind in Sync with the Subconscious, or Universal Mind.* Effective prayer takes place whenever we are thinking in the same rhythm as the Universal Mind.

As we listen to a singer singing a song—listen to the beautiful quality of her voice and how she uses it over a sustained period of time, flowing along the rhythmic current of the melodic line—we become aware of a creative rhythm and a "universal" flow that is God-like.

In a way, these qualities are the result of, or the "answer" to, prayer in their harmony with the divine Pulse of all that is (and ever will be)—God. As a singer sings, she is, in a very real sense, creating through the action of *prayer.* Singers *know* that they can sing, and when they get up to do so, they reap the fruits of their efforts.

When St. Paul said to "pray without ceasing," he meant just that; for we *do* "pray unceasingly," whether we want to or not. *As we think, we pray*—to which we might add that *as we pray, we think.*

Thinking Is Praying, and Praying Is Thinking— but at both the Conscious and Subconscious Levels. Everything We Think Is Creative, Working in the Creative Mind to Fashion a Result, Which Comes About AUTOMATICALLY.

What we want to learn, then, is how to control our thoughts, so that only good comes to us—because our subconscious mind is working nonstop, full-time, *doing what it is told.*

THINK AS A CHILD FIRST

One of the most beloved of all the stories told about Jesus concerns the time thousands of people were fed with only a few loaves of bread and a short supply of fish. Instead of having one of the learned disciples do this, *he took a boy who didn't realize that it "couldn't" be done.* This boy just did as he was told with simple, child-like faith.

This is what we mean when we say that *You Must Have a Child-like Faith:* because there will be "things" and "facts" that will turn our thought away from our faith—things that would not, however, occur to a child, who would therefore be free to do what "science" said *couldn't* be done.

That is why we must think "as a child" first and clear our mind of the prejudices and limitations of adulthood, while using *the trained intellect of our adult intelligence.* We must regain the "sense of wonder" and exercise our imaginative outlook so that we can be more accepting of what is new in our experiences—understanding it for what it is, not what we *fantasize* it is.

AN OCEAN OF CREATIVE POWER

We exist in an "ocean" of Creative Power that moves around and through us. If this were not so, then we could not create anything, directly or indirectly!

This Creative Power is God. One might say that the Word of God is but a symbol for the Power that shaped everything that is, was, and ever will be, and that this Power is functioning at all times, in everything that exists-—as shown by the changing processes of the Universe itself.

Things grow and things reshape themselves. We are in an ever-changing dimensionality that is growing upon itself, through a preset pattern and order. In our most immediate experience, all things follow the mechanics and order of the Law of Mind in Action.

Since we are a *part* of this, we are of It; and being of It, we have the same properties and follow the same laws—moving in the same rhythmic current that is the very "Growing Force" and Creative Power we call God.

To *completely* understand the essence, shape, consciousness, and Being of God would be to know *all* there is to know. Any "God" simple enough to be explained away in symbols (words) would be too small a God to have created everything that is.

WHAT KIND OF GOD *IS* THIS?

There is a Force that created the Universe. The best word for it is still *God*. God is the cohesive power that holds everything in a unified law and order; and everything is but an extension of that Creative Energy.

We are all a part of this "whole" which is God. We are a part of that which is Mind, and thus we are governed by the Law of Mind in Action. *This Being So, Prayer Must Work. It Must Work through Mind in Action.*

Why else would Jesus have said, "It is done unto you as you believe," if we did not have the power to become the *reality* of our beliefs, dreams, and fears? That is why we must learn all over again how to "be still and know."

"WHAT THEN MUST I DO?"

For this it is necessary to learn how to go within oneself with a new sense of wonder and the open-minded imaginativeness of a little child. Only in this way can what reveals itself to us be accepted without bias.

We must learn to *open our mind* and listen to the "still, small voice" of Mind in Action.

We must be willing *first to listen* before we can learn anything.

We must learn to think *positively* and *affirmatively* before we learn to pray effectively.

We must learn to KNOW that our word can and will have the desired effect every time we speak it. And the only way we can do this is to *ensure* that what we say is what we believe (what we desire), and that what we believe, we say.

THEREFORE SAY THIS:

I accept the intuition of God, which reveals to me my heritage.

I now clear my thoughts of all doubts, fears, and questions.

I know that Infinite Intelligence guides me into my true expression of life.

I know that all "secrets" for my health and peace of mind are already here and now open to me.

I and the Father are one. I know that my spoken word is now acted upon by a law of God that makes the invisible desire an accomplished event.

As we open our mind to this new awareness and look across both new and old horizons in our "imaginative" mode, we will discover the "Kingdom of Heaven" and that peace of mind which comes with the knowledge that we are one with the One Mind, which is ALL Mind.

As We Learn to Pray Affirmatively, We Will Automatically Learn How to Pray Effectively; and **Now the Time!**

CHAPTER 4

PRAYER AN *EVERYDAY* ACTIVITY

Constantly Feel the Presence of God through Prayer.

—Ernest Holmes

ONCE THERE WAS a young woman who after several years of marriage still had not been blessed by childbirth. She and her husband wanted a child very much. They had tried everything, including prayer.

One day someone said that God answered "unselfish" prayers more quickly and readily than "selfish" ones.

The young woman thereupon mistakenly changed her prayer. This time she asked that her *mother* be blessed with a *grandchild*. (Need we add that she had three sisters and two brothers?)

"IT AIN'T WHAT YOU SAY, IT'S THE WAY THAT YOU SAY IT"

Although Jesus said, "Nothing shall be impossible unto you," we would not suppose that merely *redirecting or rewording* one's desires was the secret of effective prayer.

The "Secret" Is Not So Much in What We Say as in How Convinced We Are that the Words We Speak Are True. Rephrasing the words of the prayer is not going to make it more effective.

When Abe Lincoln was told to have faith that the Lord was on his side, he replied, "I am not at all concerned about that, for I know that the Lord is *always* on the side of right; but it is my constant anxiety and prayer, that I and this nation may be on the *Lord's* side."

That is, in part, the way we all must approach prayer. We have to realize that it is up to us to become attuned to God. *This can be done by a definite process of reconditioning our mental outlook on ourselves and on the world.*

Instead of imitating our childless young woman, who

changed the direction of her wishes and desires, *We Must Create a "Sea of Positiveness" around Us*—not the familiar murky pool of negative thought and negative reactions. With God all things are possible; there are no hopeless situations—only people who have grown hopeless about them.

IT'S AN INSIDE JOB

It was Jesus who also said, "The Kingdom of God cometh not with observation, neither shall they say, Lo here! or, Lo there! For, behold, the Kingdom of God is within you." So we must first realize that when we wish to attain the Kingdom of God, or Heaven, we do so by *going with in* and starting from there.

It is through the awareness of a little child that we will recognize the Truth, which might *seem* to contradict all "scientific" law (or perhaps just our ability to understand). Then, through a sense of calm, we can look at ourselves and our world with "new eyes."

This is what Jesus meant when he stated, "Ye have eyes to see and see not, ears to hear and ye hear not." What seemed obvious to him was as good as nonexistent to those around him—because they blinded themselves, refusing to see without the prejudices of their "learning."

Since the Kingdom of God Is Within, Then That Is Where We Must Pray, and That Is the Kind of God We Must Be Praying To. And if this is where we must pray, then it must be where we are praying *all the time;* for it is within our mind that we are always thinking, contemplating, convincing.

A MAN CALLED HENRY

There was a man called Henry who sought help because even though he was successful in business and had an understanding wife and three wonderful children, he felt that everything was pointless and that he had gained all there was to gain. He felt there was nothing new for him to seek or experience or enjoy. He was bored with it all. He had had it all. Or so he thought.

At first his attitude was "I'm here only because my wife suggested that I come . . . but I don't think there's anything that anyone can do for me."

In order to convince him how wrong he was, it was suggested that he try a little experiment. He was told: "Get a camera and some color film and go out and take a score or so of the most colorful pictures you can."

He laughed at this but said he'd give it a try—though he couldn't see how this had anything to do with his problem.

A week later, he was a shocked and surprised man. His whole outlook had changed. He had discovered that in searching for colorful objects to photograph, he had started seeing everything in a new light. "Colors that I didn't even know existed . . . that I'd forgotten about . . . suddenly came to life before my eyes."

By thus experimenting, he had been forced to prove to himself that *The World Is Only What We See in It— Really, What We Look For*. Like most people, he had been living in an atmosphere of near-blindness.

ARE YOU ON "AUTOMATIC PILOT"?

Everybody has had the experience of driving along in a car, deep in thought, and suddenly finding themselves at their destination, though they were not even aware of driving or having made the right turns. They had not seen their surroundings or been aware of where they were going; they had seen the images, but their minds had rejected them in favor of the "automatic" thought-process.

This is what Henry had been doing. So wrapped up was he in his own little world, he had seen only the images of his "automatic" mental program. He thus rejected all the many other impressions in favor of those that agreed with his sad thinking.

But when he went out to take the most colorful pictures he could find, he found himself *looking for* color and *discovering* "a new world of color" that he had never been aware of.

SEE WHAT YOU *WANT* TO SEE

Now this is what we mean when we say that *Jesus Saw the World He Wanted to See.* He saw perfection; and because of his understanding of the way prayer works, he was able to project his mental world onto the world of reality. As a result, his prayers were always answered.

By his little experiment, Henry realized that it was possible to change his world by simply changing his outlook toward it. From then on, he was able to find new horizons to explore that were both endless and a "Kingdom of Heaven."

In the same way, it is possible for us all to find the happiness and fullness of life that is our birthright. And also in this same way, by looking for new horizons, seeking new understandings, and exploring new ways of looking at things, it is possible to learn the "secret" of *effective* prayer—which in reality is merely the "secret" of *experiencing only what we _want_ to experience.*

Of course, learning to pray effectively and applying what is learned can be hard work, because new mental muscles and a new mental awareness must be developed before it is possible to gain the desired response to our each and every prayer.

OUR THOUGHTS *ARE* OUR PRAYERS

Since this Kingdom is *within the mind,* it is *through the mind* that we achieve effective prayer. And it is through the *conviction* of our mind that prayers automatically obtain their results.

Thought is, therefore, the cause. The "answer" to the prayer is the automatic effect—*action and reaction.* It is a law of nature that for every cause there will always be an automatic effect. Since it is our thoughts that are in reality our prayers, then *Every Thought, Every Conviction, Every Belief That Our Mind Holds Is a Real Prayer That We Are Projecting.*

This is why it is so necessary to control our thoughts, to control our convictions, to develop new outlooks that do not include the limited, self-destructive ideas of hate, greed, selfishness—or any other emotion, action, or thing that we do don't want to experience.

Just as Henry discovered that it was possible to see with "different eyes" the world around himself just by changing his outlook, so it is possible to enjoy a wholly new life by experiencing every moment with "different awareness." *As One Selectively Sees, One Selectively Experiences anything one wishes*—by reversing one's attitude and using the *Law of Eradication.*

BOY *DOESN'T* MEET GIRL

Take the young man who sees a beautiful girl in the classroom. He would like to know her. She has personality, looks—and in his eyes is just about the most beautiful girl in the world.

There is a college dance coming up at the end of the month. He would like very much to ask her to go with him. But he is afraid.

In reality, *she* wants to meet *him,* too. But she is fearful and shy also; and though she looks in his direction every chance she gets, she just can't make herself smile encouragingly. "After all, what could he see in *me?*" she thinks.

As a result of his shyness, he doesn't ask her—because he can't imagine how such a beautiful girl could be interested in him.

Now if he had inwardly realized that there was no more reason to assume she *wouldn't* like him than she *would* like him, he would have gone to her and asked for a date. (And the same reasoning applies to her too, right?)

It's all in the way you look at it: *limited or unlimited.*
A Great Step towards Spiritual Awareness and

Effectiveness Consists in Cleansing Our Mental Attitude of All Thoughts of Limitation.

And if we can stop ourselves from entertaining thoughts of anger, greed, jealousy, sickness, bitterness, unforgiveness, and the like, we will have taken another giant step towards finding that "new outlook" which is so necessary in building an effective mental attitude.

Indeed, it's much like cleaning a machine and filling it with new oil. It runs better when overhauled. *That is what we have to do to our mind in order to pray effectively.*

WE'VE GOT TO LEARN THE *PROCESS*

We have considered the art of KNOWING and how it is so important to obtaining the answers to our prayers. But there is something else just as important as KNOWING that the thing can be done, and just as important as having the "child-like awareness" that looks at all evidence without prejudice.

That "something" is learning the *process* that overhauls our mind and prepares it for the rebuilding of a new life in which effective prayer is an *everyday* activity.

As Henry had to learn to think unlimitedly, looking for new colors and new adventures in the world around him, *We Must Learn to Use the Law of Eradication, by Consciously Dropping from Our Thoughts All the Things That Tend to Limit Our Viewpoint and Our Proper Relations with Others.*

This does not mean being "holier than thou." But it *does* mean that when we get up in the morning, instead of allowing ourselves to grumble or mutter, "Horrors! Another day!" we must learn to think "*Thank God: another day!* I'm going to enjoy *this* day to the fullest degree!"

Like a little child, we must live each day as a new adventure instead of dreading it. Instead of being blinded to the beautiful colors and activity of life, we must look with the eyes of a little child and see things with a new recognition—a new, vital, "*different*" awareness.

SPIRITUAL MIND HEALING: THE "PROCESS" APPLIED

Over the years, many have asked, *Just what is spiritual mind healing? What is it based on?*

No matter how often it is explained to them, they find it hard to accept that *It Is Not an Attempt to Materialize Spirit or to Spiritualize Matter.* It is not an effort to influence "*lower*" planes by means of "*higher*" ones.

There are many methods and many schools of thought, but all of them are basically alike in their teaching. Simply put, it is knowing that *A Definite Statement Made in Mind Produces a Specific Result in an Otherwise "Neutral," "Impersonal" Mental Field.*

There is not only a personal mind at work but, as we have already seen, a mechanical reactive and impersonal Force responding to our thoughts and convictions. This Force is governed by a law working in the same impersonal way as the law of electricity. And notice that, in its "neutrality," *It Is Not Concerned whether Our Thought Is Harmonious or Disharmonious. That's our lookout!* One might therefore call it a "blind" Force that does not *know;* it only does.

HOW THIS RELATES TO PRAYER

From all of this, we can see how *Effective Prayer Is a Definite and Consistent and Persistent Attempt to Think Straight and Logically*—because every thought and conviction that we entertain will be translated into the terms of Mind in Action, *automatically* yielding a result.

When We Learn to Control Our Conscious Mind, Our Subconscious Mind Will Learn—as an Automatic Reaction—This New Way of Thinking (and Rejecting Thoughts of Negation) with No More Conscious Effort than It Takes to Breathe.

Each day, if we only take the effort and time to reject every unhealthy thought and replace it with its healthy opposite, we will be slowly reconditioning our mental processes towards a new habit-pattern of thinking.

It's somewhat like developing a muscle. As we exercise, the muscle becomes stronger and stronger. As we learn to think without negation, the positive in our thought will become stronger, because we have been exercising our thought processes until we automatically think in different terms than we did before.

Instead of thinking limitation, *Begin Thinking Limitlessness.* How high is high? As high as your understanding will accept . . . *infinity!*

HOW IT'S DONE

How do we detach ourselves and learn this new thinking process? The answer is simple: *We Do It by Means of a Program of Willing Self-Discipline.* It is an educational process and, though not easy, it is well worth the effort it takes. Either we learn to discipline ourselves or else events do it for us. However, without discipline we will never pray effectively and consistently.

Every time we think anger or hate or critical thoughts, we should turn them around and think *peace, love, praise*. When we do this, we are flexing a mental muscle and starting the exercise of mind development.

Reversing our thinking and using the word *love* in place of *hate* is not suggesting that we adopt an artificial sweetness. When we say, "Love thy neighbor," we mean merely to give him or her the same understanding we would give ourselves: "Do unto others as you would have them do unto you."

When a person does something that we do not like, we have two courses of action to take. One is hate and the other is love.

A MAN CALLED RALPH

Everybody has had the experience of working under a person like Ralph. He believed that everyone was lazy, no good, a bad worker. He was always standing over his workers' shoulders. When any of his people made a mistake, he would become excited and blow his top. When no mistakes were being made, he went out of his way to look for some.

What was the result of his actions? What was his effect on the people who were working under him?

Nobody could think straight. Nobody could function normally. Instead of having the calmness of mind that is necessary to do a good job, they were all tense and nervous, angry and upset. Finally, most of the workers quit or were fired and replaced by others. Nobody can work under disharmony or hate.

RALPH'S OPPOSITE—EDWARD

Let us now consider Ralph's opposite—Edward. He is the owner of a very successful organization in an industry known for its nerve-racking ways and temperamental personalities—the television and motion-picture industry.

He has formed and built his business on one assumption: "If the person working for me isn't interested enough, honest enough, concerned enough to do his job to the best of his ability, then he or she doesn't belong here."

Edward expects his people to do their job honestly and competently enough not to need to be told every move to make. He always has respect for the people working for him, and as a result, they respect him. Instead of one boss and several-score *employees,* it is one *coordinator* and several-score *experts in different fields.*

Every person that Edward hires is, in his mind, expert in his or her field, deserves respect, and can be expected to do a good job, regardless of the position they hold, even down to the youngest delivery boy.

Edward is a living example of how a state of mind can project itself into the successful reality of everyday living and business. *When a Person Takes On a Truly Confident Attitude, the End Result Will Prove to Have Deserved That Confidence.*

"LOVING THE WORLD AROUND US:
SEEING WITH NEW EYES"

However, in the case of foreman Ralph, who "knew" that every person working for him was a lazy, bad worker needing supervision all the time, and who scolded for every mistake, an insecure outlook yielded an insecure result.

But if we throw aside destructive thoughts and allow ourselves to become aware of only positive actions and outlooks and begin looking for the beautiful "colors" that surround us at every turn, we will *automatically* be cleaning out our engines and re-oiling them with new friction-proof positive awareness. We will begin functioning with a smoothness that will *automatically* be rewarding and fulfilling.

Just as it is possible to walk out into the street and be blind to everything beautiful, it is just as easy to look for beauty *and find it*. That is what we mean by "*loving the world around us*" and "*seeing with new eyes*." In this way, we automatically begin *Looking for Things That Are Lovable—One Gigantic Step toward Effective Prayer.*

As we learn to see with new eyes, we will speak our word with a new authority and new awareness of what life should be and what we want to make of it.

So let's open our eyes, then! Let's look for new awareness. Let's experience new adventures *Now!*—for *Now the Time!*

CHAPTER 5

HEALING PRAYER IN THE *NOW!*

I do not know what your problems are; I do know that the time is now, and the place is here.

—Raymond Charles Barker

WHEN LITTLE JEANNIE received, at the last moment, an invitation to a classmate's birthday picnic, she surprised her mother by saying, "Golly, I can't go!" in a disappointed voice.

Knowing how much Jeannie had been awaiting the invitation, her mother asked Why? in a surprised voice. "It's gonna rain," the young girl complained sadly, "and it will be called off!"

"Don't be silly! It's sunny, and the weather man said. . . ."

"It's no use, Mommy; it'll rain!" Jeannie exclaimed in a low-pitched, trembling voice. "I *know* it will—'*cause I prayed to God that it would!*"

SWEATING THE SMALL STUFF

Though Jeannie's would seem to be a prayer of faith with a great amount of "confidence" in its being answered, this is much like the woman who wished for a grandson for her mother: *neither will be effective.* Neither is following the principles we are explaining in this book.

Some of us have the tendency to pray not for what we really want, but for a seemingly desirable "effect," which has really nothing to do with what we want in the first place. Like little Jeannie, praying for rain instead of for what she really wanted—an invitation to the party—*We Tend to Pray Only When We Want Something or Are in Trouble, and Most of the Time Only for an "Effect."*

All of us are familiar with the common cold: the "red" sore nose, the mounds of tissues, the continual coughing, the all-around discomfort. It will either get better or seem to get worse. It can be *multiplied* by our thinking or *lessened* by our thinking. It is possible to make a cold continue by just harping on how bad we feel. We say, "Oh, what a terrible cold . . . I feel horrible . . . I'm sure it's getting worse!" And if we say that often enough, it is sure to do just what we say.

As We Believe, So It Is.

If we feel that we will not get well, we will be doing nothing to make ourselves better. "Why bother? I'll be sick anyway." But when we state that *This Is Not a Necessary Condition in Our Life* and take steps to correct it, we will heal it by our convictions—followed by right actions (which are *also* the use of the Law of Mind *in Action*).

SLOW DOWN!

Sadly, there are those of us who learn the other way: we can't believe that prayer will do us any good, because the condition that makes us unhappy is "the will of God," who is "punishing" us for what we think is wrong. But let's be clear about something: *"The Only Sin Is a Mistake, and the Only Punishment Is the Consequence."* Cause and Effect.

As a person driving 90 miles an hour along a curving mountain road is likely to end up shooting over the side and dropping to his death, so it is like this when we do anything that is an ignorant, mistaken use of things, people, or situations.

But any error (mistake) *can* be corrected—something perhaps harder than doing the right thing in the first place; but it *can* be done. As our speed demon might save his life by slowing down before he runs over the edge, so we might save ourselves before we run over our "edge" and drop to personal depths below.

REVERSE COURSE!

One way of correcting a mistake is by reversing our action. As the driver stops pushing it, he is driving slowly. From fast to slow. From dangerous to safe. When we get into trouble—or, like little Jeannie, do not get something that we feel we ought to have—we should *reverse* our thinking about it.

Instead of asking for "outside" help, such as the rain in Jeannie's story, **We Must Begin by Knowing that the Condition We Find Ourselves in Is Changed from Within**.

Teenager Larry was convinced that he was quite unpopular. When asked what made him think so, he answered, "Well, I'm never invited to go to the parties with the gang at school . . . nobody comes up and talks to me . . . as far as my senior class is concerned, I just don't exist!"

When he was asked what he *did* to make himself noticed and what he *did* to become friends with his classmates, his answer was sadly revealing: "Well, I don't like to push myself on others, so I read a lot . . . if they don't want me . . . well . . . "

But his classmates, *by his own account*, didn't know he even existed! They were not aware what kind of person he was or what he had to offer. They knew nothing about him, because he had not let them look inside his "outer shell."

It was revealed to him that *he himself was not friendly to his classmates.* He lived in a world all his own—*his books and himself.*

The solution was simple enough: *Reverse Course!* All he had to do was start being friendly to his classmates, and, as a result, they would be friendly to him.

WHAT LARRY LEARNED

Larry was told that there are few people in the world who won't react to a smile; that people are not unfriendly by nature—it's just that they get wrapped up in worlds of their own. They are often as shy as the next person.

The only reason these people were "in" and Larry was "out" is that *they had put themselves into the group.* But nobody could do that for Larry. Nor is anybody going to help us unless we help ourselves.

It was suggested that he start smiling, call his classmates by name, ask them how they were; or, if that seemed too much at first, that he just say "Hello" and "Good morning."

The smile and the greeting worked for Larry. *It Was a Case of Reversing His Thinking and Actions.* Instead of feeling that everybody was against him and that nobody liked him, he had to realize that it was up to himself to convince them—show them why they should! If his nose was in a book, they wouldn't notice he was around.

His mistake was assuming that people were about to

go out of their way to bring him (or anybody else) into the group. People are usually too busy being part of the group themselves. *It is up to the individual to make his or her own moves*—not to have somebody else make them for him.

Because Larry mistakenly believed that nobody liked him, and because he did nothing to make them like him, *they didn't*. A mistake—and a result. Cause and Effect.

IT'S A LEARNING JOB

Nobody, nothing, no God makes people suffer because they have "sinned"— nor does it make some persons part of "the group" and others outsiders. *We Make Our Own Hell Right Here on Earth by Making Mistakes and Not Correcting Them.*

It is human to fumble and stumble and run up blind alleys; but it is only ignorance and stupidity to *keep* doing this in a hopeless effort to get past an impassable barrier. *When a mistake is made, it's up to us to recognize it and take the steps to correct it.*

Those who have the idea that the only time it is necessary to pray is when they are in trouble are headed for— *more trouble!* Praying is *preparing* ourselves, *learning* the way and the direction that we must go when we have to make a decision, when we have to make a move.

A track star is not made overnight, and a prizefighter would not become "World's Champion" in his first bout.

A typist must learn the mechanics of the typewriter, and which keys are which letters, before he or she will be able to type.

A musician must learn her instrument and the dynamics of music theory before she can play the violin or piano or trumpet.

A singer must learn *how* to sing before he or she can sing—and that's hard work.

This is why we must learn *to pray all the time,* which means only that we must **Think Correctly All the Time!** The truly effective prayer is only the daily application to ourselves of the words of Jesus: "All that the Father hath is mine." It is necessary to face each new day *expecting* it to give us health, happiness, and fulfillment.

WE DON'T FORCE IT, WE DON'T COAX IT

A mid-19th-century English clergyman by the name of Richard C. Trench reflected simple wisdom regarding prayer when he said, "Prayer is not overcoming God's reluctance; it is laying hold of His highest willingness."

Prayer is therefore not something we force, but a natural channel through which all things can come unto us. In other words, what Jesus said is true: "It is done unto you as you believe." As you think, so it will be. And that is why **It Is So Dangerous to Pray Only Occasionally,** betraying the fact that we have not learned how the process really works.

God gives us everything we can truly accept, and the Universe denies us nothing; but it is a waste of time to think that it will give to us because of our asking or begging. There is not a thing we can conceive of that has not already been conceived of in the Infinite Mind. An atomic force was here long before science learned how to use it; and so with all things.

NOTHING NEW UNDER THE SUN

"There is nothing new under the sun." We only discover "new" things—*new to us*—that have always been with us. We discover how to use the elements, laws, and conditions of our planet, and how to use the knowledge of the surrounding Universe gained daily by scientists. But these "new" things have been there all along.

What God has not done and is not doing now, He never did and never will do. *And Since All Things Are Possible to God, All Things Are <u>Already</u> Done.* They are there all around us—but it's up to us to discover and use them.

Healing Prayer is based on the fundamental premise that we are immersed in an Intelligence that responds to our thoughts. Since all there is and all that ever will be is already functioning in and around us, *All That We Could Ever Wish, Ever Need or Ask, Is Now Ready to Be Called Forth. What Can Be Done Has Been Done—and Will Appear in Our Experience.*

Since we are surrounded by this Intelligent Force that responds to our thoughts, then it is our very thoughts that will become causes, which in turn become effects. *Thus Our Thoughts Become Things.*

That is why a new mental awareness and attitude will cause a change in our personal world.

That is why Larry was able to become part of the group: he changed his attitude toward his friends and joined in, instead of expecting them to join *him.*

"SELECTIVE SEEING"

Once we have achieved a spiritually active center—which recognizes no limitations and sees only positive results—it is *impossible* to have anything but a healthy world surrounding us. Like attracts like!

As children often pray more effectively than adults because they are not confused by "grown-up" knowledge (which might in reality be quite false), so we can learn how to *pray* effectively through the process of *thinking* effectively. We never really stop praying; we only learn to use prayer more skillfully as our understanding of it grows.

As our knowledge grows along with the awareness of our prayer power, it is well to realize that prayer is a *natural* –not *un*natural—function. It is not something we "tack on." Again: *We Pray All the Time; Every Thought Is a Prayer.* As we believe, so it is.

When we talk about Healing Prayer, we are not talking about asking some thing or being or God to function for us. Rather, *It Is a Process of Learning the Art of Selective Seeing.*

Jesus looked at the world and saw *only what he wanted to see.* He had learned the art of *selective seeing* and as a result was able to project his vision of reality into the "real" world. *What he believed became real. He Saw the Perfect Person,* knowing it was not necessary for anyone to suffer or be sick or remain in bondage in order to be God-like. *To be God-like was to be perfect.*

PRAISE! BLESS! THANK!

Jesus Taught Praising and Blessing and Thanking God—thanking God because of what was *already* there— and he knew that it was *perfection* that was already there.

If we can do what Dickens suggested when he said, "Reflect upon your present blessings, of which every man has many; not on your misfortunes, of which all men have some," then we will be learning the art of *selective seeing*.

It was Isaac Walton who remarked, "Let me tell you that every misery I miss is a new blessing"—which is another way of looking at the positive side rather than the negative. And Shakespeare put a positive spin on a negative reflection when he wrote, "Praising what is lost makes the remembrance dear."

"CHOOSE YOU THIS DAY WHOM YE WILL SERVE"

There are two ways of seeing everything: negatively and positively. Instead of harping upon our mistakes of the past, it is just as easy to look upon the blessings and happy times.

Instead of condemning ourselves for the miseries caused by our past fumblings, it is just as easy to praise ourselves for having progressed as far as we have.

Instead of crying and feeling miserable because of something or someone lost, we should take the attitude that what we experienced and learned are things to cherish and hold dear forever..

Let's face it: *Every Minute of Our Life We Are Unconsciously Praising or Condemning.* We are forever labeling everything that takes place around us as bad or good. If we learn to become aware only of the good, rejecting the bad, we will be one step further on the way to praying effectively.

By daily watching our mind, we begin to develop the mental muscles of our awareness and thought-processes, learning to think positively and correctly. We learn to accept only what is good and harmonious and right.

It's up to *ourselves*—not an outside force or person.

As Larry had to learn to become part of the crowd by joining in, we must learn to become part of what is good by recognizing and joining in that which is positive.

If we can learn to think "What a wonderful day!" when something goes wrong or look for beauty in something seemingly ugly, we will be making the right kind of choice in developing our new mental awareness and our use of effective Healing Prayer.

USING THE LAW OF ERADICATION

Not everyone is beautiful to everyone else, yet what one might lack in physical beauty can be compensated for by an added "plus" in some other direction. As we look for this hidden "plus," we are learning to reject the negative processes of our mind and build positive ones.

Using the *Law of Eradication* in our everyday thoughts and actions might not seem the way to Healing Prayer, since we are not asking for anything. But it is not the "asking" that we are after. *We Are after a Mental Attitude That Sees Only What It Wants to Experience.* This is achieved simply by *erasing those things from our awareness that are not a part of what we wish to experience or become.*

As Larry showed interest in his classmates, they showed interest in him. As we show interest in the positive, the positive will "show interest" in us. As we recondition our thoughts so that *automatically* all that we are aware of is the positive, we will be attracting only positive actions to ourselves.

As we have seen, it is possible to regard the negative or the positive side of any thing, person, or situation. It is therefore possible to recognize, and allow ourselves to experience, *only* the positive side.

In our relations with other people, we can either take a negative approach and find ourselves unpopular, or take a positive approach, seeking friendliness, smiling, and showing interest in others. If we find ourselves "out" instead of "in," we must *join* in and show what we have to contribute to the experiences of others.

Rather than think they won't be interested in us, we should realize that they *can* become interested—if we will only give them some *positive* reason to notice us. And they will become interested if *we* show interest too.

As we can limit our social activities by limited thinking, so we can limit our whole life by a negative approach. The reason our convictions have such an influence on our lives is that we tend to evaluate our daily experience in terms of those convictions.

As we see it, so it is!

PRAYER—THE *RECONDITIONER*

If we feel limited, but determined to correct this mistaken feeling by changing our outlook and reversing our thought, we will soon find ourselves convinced of the opposite.

When we play the same CD selection over and over, we *outwardly* cease noticing it; but *inwardly* we are humming the tune with the music.

In the same way, when we say a thing over and over, understanding what we are saying, we will get to the place where we will no longer be conscious of saying it, but it will be inwardly repeating itself and becoming a major motivating factor in everything we do and experience.

Thoughts Are Things. Thoughts have energy. Brain waves are measurable. And every thought is *releasing* energy. That energy is released into the mental atmosphere surrounding our every action and activity.

Because prayer is, in reality, *thinking, Prayer Has Been Scientifically Shown to Be a Form of Energy.* Our thinking never stops, even in sleep. We are the thinker, and what we believe radiates into reality. Our prayer never ceases.

Thinking the *opposite* of the problem is what we mean by *Healing Prayer. Healing Prayer Is Nothing but Correcting Our Mistaken Outlook. As We Correct the Outlook, the Inner Experience Corrects the Outer Experience Automatically.*

So let's *eradicate* what we do not want to be a part of our lives. Let's learn to *reverse* our outlook when it is turning to the negative, the condemning, the "crying over past mistakes"—and start KNOWING that this need not be a part of our experience.

The only sin in our lives is but a fumbling mistake—*which can be corrected.* As we recondition our thought through the corrective power of Healing Prayer, we will experience a new and fuller life, which expects only the happiness that is normal and right in *Now the Time!*

CHAPTER 6

CONQUERING SUPERSTITIONS

*Wisdom, or the tide of progress . . . shall
beat against the walls of this superstition
and break down the medical opinions, lay
priestcraft low, and overflow the superstitious world with Science and good order.
Then all men will be judged by what they
know, and all can prove themselves by this
standard.*

—P. P. Quimby

IN THE DAYS of Columbus, it was considered dangerous to set sail on Friday the 13th and (before he proved otherwise) it was death to go out too far to sea; for the world was flat, and you were sure to fall off the edge—that is, assuming you survived the many sea monsters that might get you before you reached the abyss at the edge of the world. When a ship didn't return, people would nod to each other knowingly and say, "It must have gone over the edge" or "A sea monster must have gotten them!"— whereas in reality the ship had been lost to a "natural" sea disaster. So it was that these good people supported their superstitions through ignorance of what *really* took place.

HUNG UP ON THE DEVIL

Tyrone Edwards said, "Superstitions are, for the most part, but shadows of great truths." And Oliver Wendell Holmes claimed that "We are all tattooed in our cradles with the beliefs of our tribe."

But it is possible to eradicate our superstitious beliefs—as easily as King Ibn Saud of Arabia eradicated the idea in the heads of his religious leaders that telephones were the work of the Devil. The king merely asserted that if the telephone really were evil, as they believed, the holy words of the Koran would not pass over it.

By placing two mullahs (holy men) at each end of the line and having them read to each other from the holy book, he demonstrated the falsity of their superstitious belief.

ARE *YOU* SUPERSTITIOUS?

Superstition Is the Belief in Anything That Does Not Really Exist. The dictionary defines it as beliefs or practices resulting from ignorance, fear of the unknown, or trust in magic or chance—the influence of inanimate objects on human activity.

Malinda Elliott Cramer, the founder of Divine Science, put it so well when she said, "All false beliefs are suppositions that there is something that is not, or that things are different from what they are in reality and in truth; . . . these mental conditions crucify the body." How true!

Superstition has nothing to do with the Creative God of which we talk and which we KNOW. But if you fear the evil eye, the widow's peak, horseshoes, Black Friday, walking under a ladder, or black cats crossing your path, then *you are superstitious.* And the list could be greatly extended. For example:

If you fear anything associated with the number 13 or believe in lucky numbers, *you are superstitious.*

If you believe in the power of certain "lucky" charms, idols, clothes, actions, or words, *you are superstitious.*

In many primitive tribes and societies it is thought that a person should not be awakened too fast, for his soul (which they believe to be away from his body) might not have time enough to return. *That is superstition.*

However, the belief that if the tribe dances long enough before the idol of their Rain God it will rain is *correct.* (They may have to dance for several years, or for decades; but sure enough, it *will* rain—sooner or later!) If the rain comes sooner than they believe it ordinarily would, their dance has been answered (they think). If not, a sacrifice will be made to the Rain God, for which some poor sheep or dog will have to be slaughtered.

"BUT IT *SEEMS* TO WORK!"

In theory, it is possible to make *anything* happen by going through certain mumbo-jumbo and then "proving" that the antics really *do* have the "power"— because if you are sufficiently broad in your wishes and predictions, it is inevitable that they will materialize sooner or later!

Is it possible that saying "Magic Walk" will make it safe to cross a busy street? If you survive your crossings, isn't that proof that the phrase was *really* magic? But if you get killed, the reasons become numerous: either you didn't say the phrase just right; or you mumbled it; or you said it too loud; or you put the accent in the wrong place; etc., etc.

By just such "logic," superstition came into being, grew into maturity, and festered like a rotten disease. *None of This Is Belief in God or the Creative Power of the Universe!*

LET'S GET CONTEMPORARY!

The 20th century saw our first attempts to land on alien planets and explore the minute portion of the Universe that most closely surrounds us. In a new century we continue this age of science, looking into the unknown and seeking answers to the questions that have plagued humankind since it first asked the universal question *"Why?"*

Science has learned that *nothing* can be accepted at face value. Science will not tolerate superstitious belief in *anything*. It changes, grows, learns; it uses its knowledge and proves its points. It doesn't accept "the word of authority," because by tomorrow that authority might not be so. What people thought ten years ago is being questioned today and stands a good chance of being disproved tomorrow.

We live in a world that is ever looking for the answers—not faking explanations of the unknown.

"How high is up?" the little boy questions. "Ah. . . I . . . as high as the ceiling!" the flustered parent replies, in order to get rid of the inquiring young mind and get back to the urgent business of watching television.

Today, *science* is asking its own "How high is up?" and discovering that it is higher than we believed only a few years ago and that the Universe is bigger than originally thought.

This is the "New" Age, in which reasoning and thinking are considered right and normal, and the getting of the correct answers our birthright. *And in the Religion of This New Age, It Is Required that We Learn, Understand, and Reason for Ourselves.* People are referred to *themselves* to find the healing consciousness *within*. We accept no authority but the proven Truth, which is all around and through us—*an Intelligent Force that is God.*

Religion, science, and philosophy are today more and more joining hands in the fact that, through the Law of Mind in Action, it is possible to change our everyday lives, making them more plentiful and rewarding. They are all tending toward one simple philosophy of life: that our work is to find out *what* it is we believe in, *why* we believe it, and whether or not it *makes sense* and *works* in our everyday lives. *There Are No Dogmas; Only Truths—Proven!*

LET'S GET SMART!

David Hume, a Scottish historian and philosopher, pointed out that "Weakness, fear, melancholy, together with ignorance, are the true sources of superstition."

It is only through ignorance that we surround ourselves with superstitions, idols, and dogmas. In the light of knowledge, we learn to believe that God is not an individual and that "God dwelleth not in temples made with hands."

God is Creative Power. The More We Understand How to Scientifically Use the Law of Mind in Action, the More We Individualize and Personalize That Creative Power.

A symphony orchestra can weave a lace of rhythm and melody and sound, because sound already exists and we are able to perceive sound-waves. Through the method of scientific investigation, we have been able to take science, philosophy, and religion and both fuse and *use* them—*scientifically*. It is not necessary to have superstitious beliefs in things that have no real power or real effect on our everyday living; there is too much scientific evidence to prove otherwise!

FAITH IN . . . *FEAR?*

Faith in fear is just as powerful as right understanding—as powerful as using any scientific fact—because *it is a statement "entered" into the immutable Law of Principle.* Faith in an idol can have just as much effect on the believer as faith in God. But this doesn't prove that the *idol* has power, any more than dancing before a Rain God will bring rain.

Karl Menninger, a psychiatrist and one of the founders of the world-famous Menninger Clinic, called superstition a *phobia* of the anxiety or fear class. Fear is our reaction to what *might* happen, and it is our greatest adversary.

But every emotion has the capacity for showing us its *"other"* side *(It Is Two-Sided)*:

Fear / *Courage.*

Fear / *Faith!*

SUPERSTITION IS . . . *FEAR!*

A person using the words "Magic Walk" in getting safely across the street, and repeating the experiment over and over, may "prove" to himself—even though skeptical beforehand—that they really have their supposed power. The more often he is successful, the stronger his belief in their magical or "holy" power.

You have to see through the superstition, *see through the fear behind the superstition.* A snake had twined itself around a post in the middle of a primitive village, and the tribal medicine man claimed that this was a very strong sign that something terrible was going to happen.

But one young woman, not knowing too much about such things and having a tendency to see the truth regardless of what she was told, said, "That's nothing! Doesn't mean a thing! But . . . if the post had twined itself around the snake! . . . *that* would be a strong sign!"

Superstitions Could Not Exist without Fear. As we clear our thoughts of fear, we will be moving in the direction of right thinking and clear, effective mental awareness, which is the process of Healing Prayer.

Biologists have shown that fear is a "universal" emotion, common to all creatures. It is the instinct of self-preservation. A wise person once said:

> *Fear is implanted in us as a preservative from evil; but its duty, like that of other passions, is not to overbear reason, but to assist it. It should not be suffered to tyrannize in the imagination, to raise phantoms of horror, or to beset life with distresses.*

In other words, fear should not take on the traits of superstition; and when fear becomes overpowering, it does just that. Fear is false belief. Faith is KNOWING what is Truth and using it.

FEAR ONE THING!

On the United States Franklin commemorative stamp there appears the quotation "Fear to do ill and you need fear naught else."

If there were anything that we would be justified in fearing, that is it! The only thing we should "fear" (outside of fear itself) is the making of a mistake. But a mistake can be corrected; and fear can be lifted from our experience. *We Must Destroy Our Fear in Order to Pray Effectively*, because it is impossible to have faith in anything and at the same have doubt—fear—that it will not take place.

HOW TO BANISH FEAR

Preston Bradley in his book *Mastering Fear* wrote:

> *To banish fear you must look within the mind, find the cause of your fear and worry and lack of confidence. Then you must train your mental habits to a new point of view. This means substituting faith for fear, a courageous outlook for a lack of self-assurance, a positive attitude toward life for a negative.*

In simple terms: Contemplate the Opposite.

This is a reconditioning of the mind to think positively instead of negatively. It is impossible to think positively and at the same time entertain fear thoughts. *Effective Prayer Is Utterly Incompatible with Superstitious Thoughts or Convictions*. And fear is a superstition!

It is necessary to train ourselves consciously to reject fear thoughts, so that on our subconscious level we will be able to respond to the faith or KNOWING that our prayers will be answered. *It Is Impossible to Have Any Conviction that Our Prayer Will Be Answered if We Are Fearful that It Will Not Be.*

Doubt cannot he a part of faith. Doubt cannot be a

part of conviction. *Fear is not faith!* But by establishing a new thought, a new reaction, a new action, we establish a new effect.

We must channel positive convictions (thoughts without fear) into the Infinite Reservoir. Thoughts are projected energy. Energy goes someplace and does something. *Energy causes something to happen. That is effective prayer.*

As we learn to reverse our thinking, rejecting our thoughts that are limited, negative, and false, we will be learning to pray effectively.

The secret of learning to drop fear thoughts from our mind is the secret of learning *Now the Time!*

CHAPTER 7

LEARNING TO LIVE IN THE *NOW!*

The past is for us, but the sole terms on which it can become ours are its subordination to the present.

—Ralph Waldo Emerson

MANY OF US live in a web of past thoughts, experiences, fears, emotional hangovers, resentments. If this is you, then you have stopped living in the ever-present *Now!* and have begun to look to the past. Despite what you may think, you are not really enjoying life; *You Are Tending to Throw It Away.*

Others of us, young enough either in years or in experience, look only to the future—with hopes and fears. But even these people think of every future state in terms of their *past* experiences.

ALREADY DEAD

In Chapter 2 we examined the *real* nature of "old age." With some, the process actually begins when maturity is reached. A great metaphysician, Harry Gaze, once wrote, "When man reaches maturity, nature commences to bury him from the inside."

Everybody has seen the older person who believes that their world is gone. They live in old houses (which were probably old in their youth). They crowd around themselves their "treasures" of the past, which are so dear in their memory.

They live with past, dead memories. They consort with past, dead-ish people. They tend to remember only their past experiences and have stopped gathering new, present ones. They look not to the future with hope but to the merely "next" day with dread—which, they believe, brings them that much closer to the grave.

They are *already* dead.

LIKE BILL

Bill had at one time been a big executive for a large firm. In his yesterday he was a very important man, making decisions that affected many people working under him. His word was law and was respected.

During the Great Depression, the business was wiped out. Bill, well along in years at the time, discovered that his money and investments were turning into nothing. His wife died from the sudden shock of losing everything.

When at last things began again to function more normally, he was much too unsure of himself to get a job in his previous capacity. The shock of those few years had left its mark on his outlook. He found it hard to make important decisions even in the jobs he was able to get. He couldn't adjust. Finally, dropping from one job into another, he ended up as a night watchman.

Anybody who had known him when he was "top" man couldn't recognize him. Naturally, the years had lined his face; but it was not the physical features that had changed so radically.

Rather, It Was the <u>Inner</u> Features.

Instead of the assured smile and the steady handshake, the laughing, joking solid-bass voice, there was only an old, unpleasant man, bitter and lonely, friendless and unhappy. He remembered only the past glories, with no room for love and joy in the present.

THIS MAN HEARD A *DIFFERENT* DRUMMER

There was another man who had much the same fate as Bill. The 1930s Depression cost him everything, but he emerged a happy man. He forgot the past. He lived every day with a happy heart, looking for beauty and joy. He had learned that money, position, authority, and respect are but passing things that have no ultimate importance or power over one's happiness.

George Washington believed "We ought not to look back unless it is to derive useful lessons from the past errors, and for the purpose of profiting by dear-bought experience." *He Looked at the Past Only for the Purpose of Making More of the Present.*

We can let the past dominate us, as Bill did, or we can use it to point the way to a more effective living experience in the ever-present *Now!*

MEET JULIE YOUNG

Sadly, we don't seem to let our mind dwell on the present, in the ever-present *Now!—this very moment.*

As dreamers, we may be looking forward to the future with hopeful expectations. In this state of mind, all the events of the past or present seem but the gateway to the future, where we expect to find something wonderful, thrilling, and rewarding—which for some reason the past never was and the present surely isn't!

That's Julie Young. Bright, laughing, lovely. She reads movie magazines. She dreams about the time when she will know such-and-such a "celeb."

She came to Hollywood to become—*a star!* She

moves with friends whose interest is acting. Some of these people actually realize their dreams: they act every chance they get—at least practicing! They think, eat, sleep, and live acting.

But Julie never finds the time. "Oh, you don't have to do all that work!" she exclaims to her more active friends. "Just get some job at a drive-in or place where you meet the public, and where producers will discover you!"

She'll be discovered.

Maybe. Someday.

Julie has been in Hollywood for ten years, waiting to be "discovered." Some of her friends have gone on to at least a *little* glory—because they worked while she dreamed.

One of these mentioned that he would like to help her get a part. It turns out, though, that she doesn't know how to act. "She has *talent,*" was the assessment; "*but that's all.*"

Julie is still young, bright, laughing, loving—and *still* waiting to be discovered, wasting her life by dreaming, throwing away any and all chances she might have; because she has not prepared for the future.

WHERE ARE *YOU* SITUATED?

Sadly, in the process of living we somehow manage to miss the very thing itself: *the present experience.* Like Bill and Julie, we are so wrapped up in the past or the future—or both—that we have just about stopped living. If we could remember that today will be tomorrow's yesterday, and that ten years from now it will be part of the "golden" past, we would begin to value the moment and the instant we are breathing—right *Now!*

Sometimes things become valuable only when we cannot have them any more. The memories, still warm and glowing, induce us to look with biased eyes, seeing only the good and not the bad. That, in itself, isn't wrong. Looking to the past and seeing the pleasures and blessing them is right; but that is only part of it—*a very small part!*

Confucius taught people to "Study the past if you would divine the future." *Study*—but don't *live* in the past! Harry Gaze has said, "Live in the present, remembering the beauty of the past, with predominant attention on the joys and privileges of the present."

It is necessary to give up yesterday and find today. We must all give up dwelling in past wishes and desires and learn to live in the *Now! If This Is Not Done, Effective or Healing Prayer Is Impossible.* If you do not live in the *Now!* it is impossible to banish superstitious fear or to develop new mental muscles.

Those dreaming of the future are not living! Like Julie, they merely dream. But life and success are not achieved by dreams alone. It takes more. *You Can't Live in the Past! That Is Gone and Finished. You Can't Live in the Future! That Has Not Yet Come.* Each day must be a new experience. We must seek a *new adventure.*

IN NO TIME AT ALL

A person can enjoy living at 90 or 20, at 3 or 50. There is no such thing as time—*or old age.* The dictionary defines *time* as a fundamental *conception*, involving recognition of the ideas of *before* and *after, past, present,* and *future,* in a sequence of events.

Albert Einstein said that there was no such thing as "absolute time" (which has a flow and set rhythmic pattern that starts at one place and ends at another). In his Theory of Relativity, he said that time was much like the sense of color in the human being—only a form of *perception.* As color could not exist without an eye to see it and a brain to "make" it, time could not exist without a mind to record it or shape it or break it up into an order of events.

Time is simply the perception, concept, or selector that, as Thomas Edison's assistant Ray Cummings once said, "keeps everything from seeming to happen all at once." This is proven by the fact that time is *relative* to all things and events and experiences. During the experience of joy, time quickens. During grief, it seems to be delayed.

"When you sit with a nice girl for two hours," Einstein explained, "you think it's a minute. But when you sit on a hot stove for a minute, you think it's two hours. That's relativity."

SAME GOES FOR *AGE*

Francis Bacon pointed out that age is only the measure of experience: "A man that is young in years may be old in hours, if he has lost no time." Time is the file-box of experiences that we build into our memory banks for accessing when needed. *Age Is an Illusion* that the more "experienced" make too much of!

The experiences of the past have no more effect on

our lives than we let them have. Our sad friend Bill could have had an exciting life filled with love and joy—but for his mental attitude, which saw everything only in terms of past glories and defeats.

He could have changed his living experience simply by changing his mental awareness and outlook. Instead of looking back and feeling cheated, he could have looked to the future with contentment by expressing himself creatively in the ever-present *Now!*

We are just as capable of right action today as we were yesterday or will be tomorrow. *It Is Never Too Late to Change Our Lives, Our Mental Awareness, and Our Thinking.*

It is never too late to start developing new mental muscles.

It is never too late to drop fears, anxieties, and superstitions from our awareness.

Nor Is It Ever Too Soon!

Anyone who believes he knows it all has stopped growing. Anyone who feels "old," tired, and outdone—who believes he has seen and experienced all of his life—has stopped living. A person living in the past is not progressing; he is stagnating. And a thing that stagnates is in a slow state of decay. It is certainly not living.

We Are No Older in Mind than We Were When We Were Born; the only measure of "age" is our experience. The active mind is not interested in past deeds but only in those to be done *today*. Yesterday, the present, and tomorrow all blend into the ever-present *Now!*

HOW ARE WE PROCESSING OUR EXPERIENCE?

Experience directly affects our thoughts, actions, and reactions. A man who as a child was supersensitive and couldn't take the ribbing of his friends when he fumbled in football games could very easily learn to hate sports. There is no good reason for him to hate them, but in his mind's filing system there are cards which say that games are emotionally painful experiences. So he hates sports because he dislikes pain.

Perhaps a young girl eats too much candy one day and gets sick. From then on she doesn't like candy, ice cream, cake, or other sweets. She should learn not to eat *too much* candy instead of not liking *any* of it because "it" made her sick. That would be learning from the past to profit the future.

Like a little child, we must look on each instant as a new adventure. As adults, **We Must Look Outward from Experience,** learning from past adventure. Then, as "trained" adults, having learned from past mistakes, we move into the future through our actions of today.

The person who uses time *that* way to the best of his or her ability will find in life all that he can ever use or need or want.

READY?

Are we willing to turn our back on yesterday—*and tomorrow too?* Willing to forget every unhappy experience? Willing to live today, *Now!*, and not in the past or future?

Everybody makes mistakes. We all fumble and do stupid things. We are only human; we are experiences of Mind being aware of its existence and surroundings. And it is perfectly right to regret those mistakes.

Once we *do* regret them, however, we will start doing something about them! The very act of regretting our mistakes and wasted time will make us value what remains to us and get us to use it to the best of our ability.

We must not condemn the past; we must *praise* it for what it taught us. Then look to *Now!*—and *live!*

But if such thoughts come to *plague* us, we must finally refuse them, reject them, and think the opposite. ***Until We Can Do This, We Will Never Pray Effectively.***

Longfellow said: "Nor deem the irrevocable past, as wholly wasted, wholly vain, / If rising on its wrecks, at least to something nobler we attain!"

Look to every moment as a priceless gem, forgetting concepts of time and space and age. Then we know that all there is and ever will be, can be ours in ***Now the Time!***

CHAPTER 8

HOW MUCH ARE YOU WORTH?

You are the only creature on this plane who was created to work CONSCIOUSLY WITH GOD!

—John Lee Baughman

EVERYONE HAS HEARD, read, or said that, chemically speaking, the human body is worth just a few dollars—a true statement. That is the "market value" of the material that makes up our bodies.

But what "market" are we talking about? In war, a human life becomes worth just the cost of a little powder and a small chunk of lead. Medical institutions will give $100 or more for the right to use a person's body after they have passed on.

But perhaps we are *differently* materialistic, measuring everything in securities and positions. "You're only worth as much as your bank account": we've all heard that before. With it may go a huge office, big house, expensive car—and a pat on the wallet.

The ambitious person feels that his worth is measured by his "position." He might not be making too much money (yet), but because of *him*, other people are kept "on their toes"! He rates things by the *power* a person has over others. "Why, if anything happened to *me* . . ." This soul is a great micro-manager. Without him there to make every decision, the sky would fall. Nobody else is able (translate *trusted*) to do what he can do.

Conflicts in understanding *worth* and *value* have raged since time immemorial. Writers of both fact and fiction have covered the subject unto weariness. It has had us all questioning just what our worth is; but for what purpose? To change it? Raise it? And why? To question? To wonder? To doubt? To dream or wish?

PINNING WORTH TO *EFFECTS*

When we are sick, our greatest "worth" is health; when we are jobless, a job. When we are homeless, "worth" is a home. The mistake inherent in viewing *worth* this way is that it can become a trap. *Instead of Looking for the Cause of Our Troubles, We Attempt to Find a New Effect.* Yet once the cause is found, the effect is on its way to changing. And once the cause is corrected, the *effect* is corrected. Automatically!

Jack Jones and his family prove this. They keep moving from one house to another in their search for happiness. (They place a mental price-tag on a house as the symbol of happiness.) They search for another and yet another house, with new surroundings, fooling themselves into thinking that a new *house* is a new start, a "new lease" on life.

Their mistake is in thinking that a new house or position is itself a *value*, e.g. happiness. They will probably go on all their lives buying, collecting, and searching anew—and all this on a plane that has nothing to do with what they *really* desire or want.

What is this, in fact, but an escape from their real problem: *lack of happiness*—?

"ATTENTION, SHOPPERS!"

Sorry, there are no "specials" on happiness today! Happiness is not bought; it is worked for. Happiness is an awareness, a contentment, a knowingness of the good that we do, feel, express, in the creative outgoingness of our nature.

Happiness comes in many ways, as when we realize that, being one with God, we are equal with all persons. Being of One Mind and having the divine powers that are all around us to use makes us as "equal" with all others as it's possible to be.

Freedom, we say, is our birthright. Liberty, we say, is something that all people can have; but do they? We must learn to be *free* of all doubts, fears, prejudices, hates, and mental dogmas. *That is liberty!*

Freedom and liberty are simply that state of being we attain when we have learned how to use the *Law of Eradication. Once This Law Has Been Used and Lived by, We Have All the Freedom and Liberty Anyone Could Ever Attain*—an ability to erase all things that we do not want to experience.

If we want a plentiful supply of all things good, then we must erase from our awareness all things that are negative and limited, for these have nothing to do with our true worth.

WE ARE AS WORTHY AS WE MAKE OURSELVES

But not in the material "market value" of our body; not in the amount of stocks and securities we have amassed; not in the job, position, or power we may have. Our value comes not in what we own, what we collect, what we seek or have—or have become or will become—but rather in our personal output in the world around us.

How much of the self do we express? How much do we attempt to use the creative side of our nature in a *con-*

structive way? (It is only too easy to be "creatively" *destructive!*)

What are the reactions of friends and outsiders to our words and actions? How much *of good* are we adding to the world? Here lie the determinants of our worth as individuals, as creative channels. And here we find what decides our value to the world around us.

HOW TRUE WORTH BECAME *A NATION*

What must have been the early colonists' thoughts when they decided to start a new nation? What were their dreams and reasons, their beliefs and reactions to the world around them? It all must have had a great deal to do with worth—*self-worth.*

No doubt they wanted freedom for personal reasons; "giving to the world a new nation devoted to the equality and freedom of all men," etc., etc., was probably only a *result.* Indeed, they wanted something that the rest of the world could not give them.

They landed on new soil and saw before them, first of all, the very freedom of nature itself—the "natural" freedom that all creatures should have. They saw the possibility of carving a new concept that in fact was as old as the Universe, the possibility of bringing to the Earth a place where people of all nations could come and be free and equal.

The colonists broke away from the old and brought forth the new, carrying with them what they had conceived *as ideas* in their home country. *Ideas Are What*

103

Brought Them to the New World. And this is why they were willing to die for their new-found freedom.

THESE WERE THEIR CRIES—THEIR "PRAYERS"

"Give me Liberty or give me death!" This is, when you stop and think about it, the cry of all men and women. As for the colonists, they fought, struggled, and died for what they desired—Liberty! Freedom! A state in which they could exercise their divine right to think, speak, believe, and live as they wished.

" *We hold these truths to be self-evident, that all men are created equal; that they are endowed by their Creator with certain inalienable rights."* These rights included "life, liberty, and the pursuit of happiness"—the pursuit of one's own personal form of happiness, not that of some king, dictator, or bureaucrat. *The right to make our own decisions.*

The first Congress in 1775 expressed the desires and the rights which this nation would recognize as its very foundation. The free expression of self is but the evolution of Spirit. Evolution is a planned program for the unfolding of divine ideas on the human level—the emergence of what we *can* be out of what we have *believed* ourselves to be.

Men died so that we could have the right of *personal* liberty, whatever other liberties we might have added. They fought for our right to think for ourselves, to express our own thoughts when and where we wish—and for the right to make our own mistakes.

It is interesting, therefore, to examine the forging of

our American nation in the light of what this book is all about: *Clearing Our Thought in a Climate of Freedom So that We Can Make Choices Which Will Become Effective Prayer—That Is, Will Materialize in Our Experience as That Happiness Which Is the Object of Our "Pursuit."*

ARE WE "LOYAL" TO LIBERTY?

Based on the foregoing, we can easily see how many of us Americans actually *betray* our heritage! That is, we betray our very *liberties*—because we have not learned how to use them *personally* (regardless of what we think we're doing as an electorate, as members of political parties, etc.). We waste our time on superficial effects (some of them political) without making an effort to correct our *personal* errors of the past in order to attain a freer, more secure future.

Ours are liberties worth dying for. And we have seen that the colonists didn't consider that too great a price to pay for securing their self-worth.

But we must learn to be free of all doubts, fears, prejudices, hates and mental dogmas!

That is liberty.

True freedom and liberty are simply that state of being which we attain when we have learned how to use the *Law of Eradication*. Once this law has been used and lived by, we have all the freedom and liberty it's possible to attain—an ability to erase all things that we do not want to experience.

If we want a plentiful supply of everything good, then

We Must Erase from Our Awareness All Things Which Are Limited and Negative.

That is what we mean by liberty. *That* is the liberty worth dying for.

HOW MUCH ARE *WE* WORTH?

Then how much are *we* worth? Worth the amount of creative energy we expend? Worth the amount of happiness we put out so much energy for? The money, position, or power we try to gather around us? That depends on our point of view, on our willingness to be a free channel for expressing the divine creative power that is all *around us* and flowing *through* us and working automatically *for us.*

That is why healing power is *normal.* Natural. Not *ab*normal or freak occurrence or something "added" unto us. *It Is Merely Using the Creative Power in Our Everyday Activity.*

It is the true proof of our worth.

IF WORTH=WEALTH, WHAT *IS* WEALTH?

Speaking of *worth*: do we equate this with *wealth*, and wealth with *competition*?

We have to ask ourselves what our wealth *really* consists in—exactly for *what* we may be struggling and competing.

And why <u>are</u> we struggling?

Do we really want what we are struggling and competing for? Or is it just that we want others to see what we have?

Terry is like that. When she dates someone, it's not

106

because he is someone she necessarily likes. Rather, it's someone she thinks will help to show off her popularity. A *trophy* date.

That would be Frank.

The irony is, Frank *is* genuine "trophy" material: he's the most popular boy in school—all the girls want to go out with him—because he's the hero of the football team.

This is not the right kind of competition. This is not competing to better oneself. *This is pure ego-boosting!*

SHE HEARS A DIFFERENT DRUMMER

Jill is refreshingly different. Confident of herself, Jill doesn't have to be seen with the most popular boy in class. She knows what she wants and knows how to go about getting it. But what *does* she want?

Well, she wants to *enjoy* herself. Nothing wrong with that! She also wants to *express* herself: she wants to share experiences with boys and girls she likes (no need to get involved with the others). She wants to share *herself.*

She goes out with a boy because she likes him, not because being seen with him will make others look up to her in surprise and envy.

Terry is like the person who has to have a *bigger-*screen TV (even if unaffordable), not to be "left out." To see television better? No; to *look* better—a status thing. Only a person unsure of herself resorts to this kind of "competition."

It *is* wonderful to have a big-screen TV. It *is* wonderful to have a big, expensive car. *But at what price? And for what reason?*

For *happiness?* Happiness does not lie in *merchandise* but in *mind.* *When We Are Content, Sure of Ourselves, Doing and Expressing Creatively, Giving to Others and Receiving from Others the Greatest Gift of All—Self-Expression—We Are Not Bothered about the Size of Our TV or the Dollar Value of Our Car.*

WE *ALREADY* "HAVE"

Instead of worrying if we have all the things that our friends have, trying to "keep up with the Joneses," we must realize that we have the same creative power they have and the same divine right to use it; we have the same freedom of thought and the same right to happiness.

We don't need bigger and more expensive *anything* in order to be happy or creative—or to establish our worth or wealth. "All that the Kingdom hath"—*that* is what we have, and *it is all we will ever need.* Yet if we lost every material thing we possessed, what would be our reaction? Fear? Or would we *still* be sure of ourselves?

If we realized where *true* happiness lay, we would not find material wealth necessary in order to get there. We should be able to enjoy life regardless of the props (or lack of them) we might have. We have only to realize that what any one person *truly* has, *we* have: the same divine power, freedom, and liberty. What we had at birth we *still* have now; what we had before we gained material possessions we *still* have now: Mind. Liberty. Freedom.

Wealth Is an Outgrowth of Ourselves—not an end, or a means to an end. As we use the Creative Power within us, we automatically draw things to us.

Cause and Effect. Action and Reaction.

This is the Law of the Universe, of Nature, of Mind in Action—of God.

THE "GOLDEN RULE" IS *ALSO* PART OF IT

"Do unto Others As You Would Have Them Do unto You": that too is part of our use of the Creative Power—in the same way that you would have others use the Creative Power with you, especially *in their thoughts of you.*

We would rather see a smiling face. *So would they!*

Our ability to creatively express the Power in an effective way, so that it radiates before us and signals happiness, contentment, and love, comes from looking *within* our awareness and KNOWING that it's *Now the Time!*

CHAPTER 9

THE POWER OF THE SUBCONSCIOUS

Our relation to the subconscious is the key to all that we are or ever can be.

—Thomas Troward

IN THE PREVIOUS eight chapters we have seen how we are all of us creative, thinking beings who have the power and the ability to change our lives by using the *Law of Eradication*. We have learned how it is possible to eradicate from our awareness what we don't want to experience. Now the next step is the rebuilding of our world. We have erased the old, and now we are ready to build the new. *Now Is Indeed the Time!*

OUR FORCE-FIELD

We have become aware of that inner power which we call Mind, Intelligence, Spirit; and we have also become aware of our *true* relationship to God.

It is the divine "scheme of things" that we are thinking beings and our thoughts project into a field of energy that is creative *by responding to our every conviction*.

We think all the time—even in our sleep. As Eugene Del Mar put it: "The subconscious is always awake, even when the conscious sleeps." We cannot stop thinking, because *It Is Our Very Nature to Think*. Thinking is our awareness of, and reaction to, all the things around us. *Thinking Is What Distinguishes Us from Everything Else in the Universe*. This is what the Bible means when it says that we are fashioned in the image and likeness of God. *God Is a Thinker, and We Are Thinkers*. Think about it!

We now realize that the very field or atmosphere surrounding our mind is itself an active force and that *This Force Goes the Route of Our Convictions and Does Things with Them*.

READY . . . SET . . . GO!

Now we are ready to put this force into action in a *desirable, effective* way—so that it will create only those things that we want to happen in our experience. Every thought, every reaction that we have, has its *emotional* counterpart; and *this* is the "warhead" of that thought, that reaction, that conviction.

For example, persons whose loved ones hurt them respond to *two* levels of awareness. First, they are aware of something like actual *physical* hurt. They are "stunned," "staggered," "wounded," "heartbroken," etc., when they recognize what has happened.

Then they have an *emotional, feeling* reaction (often expressed as *"hurt feelings"*), and *This Emotional Reaction Will Decide the Intensity and Degree of Energy They Will Project into Their Mental Atmosphere.*

If the emotion is anger, hate, fear, terror, or pain, the mental projection will be *negative.* (We need not mention that the reverse also holds true, in the same "law"ful way: if a loved one does something that expresses love, affection, trust, esteem, etc., the emotional reaction will be of the same kind, a thing of *positive* nature.)

THE SUBCONSCIOUS "BRIDGE"

What, where, and how does this emotional energy project itself? What is the route it travels?

The Subconscious Mind Is the Bridge. In fact, all reactive emotions and feelings depend on the subconscious mind. And notice that creative persons of all kinds use the subconscious mind—artists, writers, actors, musicians:

they have to. You may not have known it, but so do successful businesspersons.

It is well known that if creative writers had to depend only on "inspiration," they would get almost nothing done. *Professional writers never wait for inspiration.* They train themselves so that when they sit down at the keyboard they automatically "call on" the subconscious. *There* lies their inspiration!

Actually, the subconscious is the only truly *creative* thing within us. *It Is the Bridge to the Infinite Intelligence, the Creative Power of the Universe—across Which the Creative Energies Enter the Conscious Mind—Our Awareness.* They come one at a time or in armies; but it is only over the subconscious "bridge" that the conscious mind is able to be aware of so-called inspiration.

Our thinking, conscious mind is the reasoning center of our physical awareness. It reacts to outside stimuli. But it is through the *subconscious* mind that we become *creative beings,* functioning in a *creative field.* The subconscious bridges the gap between the reacting conscious mind and the One Creative Mind.

WE ARE NOT *CREATORS* BUT . . . *CREATIVE*

We are not creators. Our mind does not *create* anything; *We Only Discover and Use.* But we *are* able to use the Creative Power, which does (and always will) respond to our beliefs, convictions, desires, feelings, and thoughts.

We are creative beings only in so far as we *consciously* use the Creative Power at our disposal. But without the subconscious, we would be nothing much more than reactive, mechanical machines—without free will or creative ability—merely reacting automatically to outside stimulation.

The subconscious is therefore the bridge to the Infinite Creative Force of the Universe. It is the factor or ability—call it what you will—that makes it possible for us to be creative at all. Our conscious mind is but an instrument that creates through the power which the subconscious taps. *Our Job Is to Learn How to Consciously Use and Control the Subconscious.*

AND HERE *NOW!* IS THE KEY

We have already seen the central role of emotion. Now consider emotion in this revealing way: emotion is *awareness* reacting on *other* forms of awareness and other "outside" physical actions and stimuli. This is how we end up with *two* reactions to a physical stimulation: physical reaction and emotional reaction.

Therefore since the physical is subordinate to the emotional, *We Can Actually Correct, Channel, and Redirect the Emotional, Thereby Causing a New, Different, "Healing" Effect in the Physical. This Is the "Secret" of All Healing Prayer!*

The emotional reactions of our conscious mind send energy into the subconscious, leaping across the bridge into this creative field, which responds automatically—*negatively or positively.*

Since the physical world is subordinate to the mental, this "event" in the *mental* (creative energy) affects the *physical*—automatically!

Thus, in order to experience and enjoy a well-balanced and happy life, *We Must Learn to Control Our Emotional Responses.*

And always remember: our emotional responses are controlled by the *intellect*—the conscious, thinking, analyzing, selecting, reacting awareness.

CONFLICTED?

Some people have a conflict between the emotional and the intellectual. That is, they *realize* what is right and what is wrong (at least for them) but find it hard to control their emotions. In other words, *they give in to their emotional reactions.* Often they even *refuse* to practice self-control.

Control is gained by perceiving the outside world with new eyes and new beliefs—a new awareness.

A person living in a mental awareness of love will find it hard to respond to hateful stimuli and "outside" actions. Those who say something spiteful, cruel, angry, or critical will elicit no negative response from one who is mentally well adjusted.

The well-adjusted person "turns the other cheek" in the sense that he or she mentally "blesses" the other person, giving the same understanding he or she would like to get and realizing that the person was reacting to something within *himself* that didn't come from love. *The Well-Adjusted Person Does Not React to the Negative, Preferring to Ignore It—and to Respond as though to Its Opposite!*

Uncontrolled emotions cause chaos, confusion, and conflict in our mental atmosphere—in our subconscious mind—and therefore in the Creative Energy surrounding us. If the chaos is wild enough, overpowering enough, it will affect not only ourselves but others too.

Each of us has had the experience of being in a crowded room where everyone was having a good time, when suddenly everything seemed to go flat. There was a murmur, and things abruptly slowed down and got heavy.

The reason? A new person had just walked in whose every movement and facial expression bespoke a single emotion: depression. He was so negatively depressed that the emotion projected like an electric charge. The mood began to shift to others—at least to the susceptible.

WE *MUST* LEARN CONTROL

It Is Necessary to Learn Control over Our Mental Atmosphere. Without controlling our thoughts and our feelings, we will never pray effectively. We will never learn how to use the *Law of Eradication.* We will never be able to change our lives. We will never gain a new, fulfilling happiness which it is our right and freedom to have.

Sound dire? Nevertheless *it's so.*

We have the power to change our lives. We have the power to erase from our experience what we don't want to experience. This is the Creative Power that is all around us and flowing through us—*and We Can Use It!* If this were not true, we would *never* be able to express ourselves creatively.

But we must first learn to control our mind! We must learn to control our *emotions*—for it is through our emotional responses that we project the subconscious nega-

117

tively or positively into the Infinite Creative Force.

We learn to control our conscious mind and emotional reactions by learning to reverse our thoughts. *We Must Reverse Our Thought about, and Our Reaction to, Anything That Is the Reverse of Perfection and Right Action*—because, as Malinda Elliott Cramer wrote a century ago, "Man could not exist as the reverse of God."

REVERSE THE REVERSER!

How high *up* is, depends on how *low* low is. It may also depend on where you are standing. We must have something with which to *compare* the emotion or thing or whatever it is. Without joy, we would not know sorrow. Without hate, we would not know love.

When we are sick, if we will *Reverse the Reverser* by remembering and realizing how well we felt before we became sick, we will begin to restore our awareness of the health we felt—and with that awareness, we will rightly expect to see our health return.

When we experience personal loss, we must realize that there is nothing lost in God's world—only a law of circulation at work. When there seems to be lack in our lives, we must right then and there plan on what we would do with *more than enough!*—and then proceed to take action *to get more!*

Nothing happens only by wishing; even true, scientific prayer must be followed by *action. Prayer Is Only a Means to Prepare Ourselves to Take What God Has Already Given Us.*

When we are unemployed, we must realize that there

is someone in the world who is going to be our next employer. We must bless that person, whoever he or she may be—*and then go and look for the job!*

It is only through lack of faith that we don't take action. All the while, God is directing us—and when we say God, we mean the All-Knowing Intelligence, the Intelligence Within, that "still, small voice" of the subconscious directing us.

That is when we should move. Not for us to sit static! We don't just lie around and pray. Praying is a way to help find the answer to our problem in the subconscious mind. ***But It Is Then Up to Us to Help Ourselves.*** That is the meaning of the saying "God helps those who help themselves."

The *right way is right there* for us to go; *but it is up to us to go!*

ONCE MORE, WITH FEELING: *REVERSE THE REVERSER!*

Reverse any thought, idea, or experience that might come across your awareness which is trying to limit your life and outlook on the world around you.

Reverse the Reverser (the negative imperfection). We control our mind and emotional responses *by not reacting to the negative.* We become blind to all things that are disharmonious (negative), while at the same time we become aware of the harmonious (positive).

Believe It or Not, It's That Simple!—and the consequences for our lives are simply *staggering!*

When we leave home in the morning and allow ourselves to be on the lookout for beauty and all things lovable, we *automatically* stop looking for the ugly and negative. Instead, we become aware of *only the good*—not the bad.

We recognize only the lovable and mentally reject the unlovable. This is the art of reversing our thoughts and emotional reactions—*reversing the reverser.*

When a person does something that seems wrong in our eyes, we must ignore that action and make a conscious effort to see only the things in that person which are good and God-like—the *reverse* of our wrong seeing.

Anyone can do this. We have the freedom and choice. And we *can* tell wrong from right. It's up to us to look only for the right, good, beautiful, lovable, true. It's up to us to erase all things that are "impossible" from the *God-like possible*—drop from our awareness all things that seem imperfect.

YOU'RE THE ONE!

You are the only one who can do it! Nobody else can do it for you. And that is the simple principle of controlling your mind and your emotional responses. *Simplicity itself*—just looking at the world with eyes of love, instead of with eyes of hate.

It *is* simple, once you know how. It is the *learning* how that takes time and effort. It is through exercise that we develop the new outlook, the new awareness—the new happiness.

If we want happiness, then this is the work we will have to do for it.

It's worth it!

AND NOW *IS* THE TIME!

As you impress upon your mind the following affirmations and statements, you are releasing the energy of harmonious living into action.

This can be the beginning, the start towards a new life.

I clear my mind of all thoughts of limitation.

I am aware only of that God-like quality within me which recognizes love, beauty, and harmony.

I know that from this moment on I am aware of only what is God-like.

I move through my day KNOWING that I attract, see, and express only love, beauty, and harmony. Therefore, I automatically attract to myself only qualities, emotions, and reactions consistent with these qualities.

Let's know that all these things are true. Let's know that they are a part of our being, living, and experiencing—for *Now the Time!*

CHAPTER 10

THE POWER OF GIVING
AND RECEIVING

Never examine the teeth of a gift horse.

—St. Jerome

IN OUR SEARCH for personal abundance and the happiness of life that is ours for the *accepting* (and not for the *asking!*), we are prone to ignore some special blessing that may be offered to us. The hardest thing in the world is to accept a gift, be it health from God, Love from our family, respect from our associates, or just "Let me take you out to lunch."

"WHAT'S THE CATCH?!"

Instead of being able to receive lovingly, we have an automatic reaction to wonder why this or that person is *giving* such-and-such. We find it hard to keep from reacting suspiciously. We begin to wonder about their motives— what they might want from us. But a person might be giving just for the joy of *giving*. We forget that just as *we* enjoy the spirit of giving, others like to give to *us*. As we give, we receive.

Giving can be a spontaneous expression that generates an inner feeling of joy, happiness, and importance. In rejecting a gift from another, we are putting up a solid brick wall of resistance to the Love that they are trying to express.

But that's not all! By the very action of giving, *we receive*. By the very action of receiving, *we give*. It is an endless circle. So if we refuse, we are resisting this circle, we are putting a block in the Law of Circulation.

THE LAW OF CIRCULATION

The Law of Circulation is the law of giving and receiving. It is the law that brings order and balance to the

Universe. We can't seem to accept the idea that all is subject to the law of movement, change, and growth.

Everything in the Universe moves in circles. Einstein tells us that even light and space bend back upon themselves. The only movement that can be eternal is *circular*. So the vow of love everlasting is symbolized by the wedding ring, which has no beginning and no end.

As We Give, We Receive. As we express creatively, we receive the rewards of that expression. Jesus said, " Give and unto you shall be given good measure pressed down and running over."

But giving and receiving covers more than just the expression of *material* giving and receiving. There is the giving of praise—the gift of being able to enjoy and be grateful for those things and people that are around us. We can accept and we can give. We can take what the world has to offer and at the same time give to the world what we can offer. *It's the Law of Circulation!*

An old Jewish legend about the origin of praise is one of the best stories concerning this necessary ingredient to the fulfilling of our lives. After God had created humankind, says the legend, He asked the Angels what they thought of the world He had made.

"The only thing lacking is the sound of praise to the Creator," the Angels replied. So God created music—the voice of birds singing, the murmuring of the ocean, and the throb of melody planted in the human heart. The sound of praise: *the sound of looking to the good and seeing it and hearing it and praising it.*

GIFTS OF LOVE, PRAISE, FORGIVENESS

To truly love, one must love *all* things. When love is limited, it is self-centered. Being self-centered, it does not express itself to the fullest. The gifts of love, praise, and forgiveness are the God-like qualities within all of us. *As We Love, We Are Loved. As We Praise, We Are Praised. As We Forgive, We Are Forgiven.* As we give love, praise, and forgiveness, we receive those same qualities from others and the world around us.

If we walk out onto the street *looking* for love, *looking* for beauty, *looking* for things to praise: *we shall notice and enjoy the things we are seeking.* And if we look for hate, fear, and the negative, we will only be aware of those defects.

We are speaking here about the ability to experience the things that are God-like and that are expressing the qualities of Love and Beauty. God is a presence full of warmth, color, light, and awareness. God is all there is and in everything that is. The world is actually full of Love and Beauty. *It is up to us to look for it. And as We Look for It, We Are Automatically Using the Law of Eradication.*

It has been said that "the lives of all of us would be more abundant if more men and women desired to experience the abundance of life." The biggest block to receiving is *holding*. To be functioning in harmony with the universal rhythm and flow of Nature, it is necessary to reflect those qualities that accord with the Universe. The nature of the Universe is to circle back upon itself. *As you give, you receive.* "Give and it shall be given unto you." Those of us who wish to be loved must express love.

Those who wish to receive must give.

And those who enjoy giving must learn the art of receiving!

ONCE AGAIN: REVERSING THE REVERSER

What we see in others and the world around us is but a mirrored reflection of our mental attitude. If we seem to be surrounded by the ugly, unpleasant, destructive, then our minds are reacting to *those* emotions and ideas. But if we change out mental attitude so that it reacts only to Love, Beauty, and the Constructive, then *those* are the results and effects that we shall experience.

This reversal of the thing that causes everything to appear reversed from what is God-like and Love is . . . *Reversing the Reverser.* (Remember?)

Thoughts are things. Our only power is the energy we release through our thoughts; and it is released with *every* thought. Therefore we can control this energy only as we learn to control our thought—scientifically.

It takes a recognition that there is a spiritual Mind Power within us which, if recognized, will enable us to reverse course and escape to a New Reality. This is how we bring ourselves back to the sanctity of accepting Love as a principle of happiness, of contentment, of right life and living—indeed, *of faith.*

Faith in God.
Faith in ourselves.
Faith in the Intelligent Power Within.
Faith that we are intelligent beings.
Faith that we can and do *think* and *reason*.

SHEER INTELLIGENCE!

Of course, these are all ways of saying the same thing: that "I and the Father are one"; that "I and intelligent thought are one." What more can we have? What more could we need? *Nothing!*

There is that within all of us which is intelligent. It is the very spark of reason, which all of us are able to use. By thinking, we set into action a series of ideas, thoughts, concepts that are linked together and continue on into Infinity, never stopping and always occasioning new ideas, thoughts, and concepts. Each thought leads into the next, and every new one bridges another, like an endless, ever-growing chain.

As when a pebble is thrown into a pool of still water there follow endless ripples, each beginning from the center and exploding outwards in a great circle that is ever-enlarging, each new thought begins a new rippling in the pool of our minds, creating its own effects within our subconscious and outward through our actions.

It is impossible to take physical action without first giving thought to it. You might even say that each thought has its counterpart in the physical world. The thought might be hate, fear, anger, terror—and the action might only be the nervous tightening of a facial muscle. But there will always be a physical response of one kind or another following upon our thought. *Thoughts Are Things!* And actions are the *re*actions of the physical to our thoughts.

MIND IS THE MAKER

Nothing happens or can take place without the Law of Mind in Action. This is a mechanical and automatic mechanical reaction: the thought first and then the action; cause and effect; action and reaction. All things begin in Mind and well outward, causing effects wherever they make contact. And as with water, when the "rippling" hits an obstruction—such as a rock—it causes counter-ripples that return to the sender like sound waves bouncing off an object and returning, or like radar bouncing and returning.

Thought waves also "bounce back" and return. As you send thought outward, it comes back to you. If the thought is destructive, the "bounce-back" will be destructive. *As you give, you receive.* Whatever action, thought, emotion projects as a result of our mental attitude will create an automatic effect on all things around us.

Therefore, since it all begins within the mind, that is where we must seek the cure for an ailment that we have. In other words, we must learn *controlled thinking*. *And We Must Learn to Make a Decision—and Keep It.*

IT BEGINS WITH A DECISION

We must determine to "decide" to do something. We can decide anything we want to. We have the power and liberty of free choice. It is up to us to make the decision to clean up our mental machinery and re-oil it so that it will be working more smoothly and harmoniously with the Universal Rhythm of all things. We must use the Law of Mind in Action in a scientific way so that it is working *for* our happiness and not *against* it.

The Law works impersonally. It responds to our thoughts automatically, without any interest in what the thought was or the outcome of it. Since every time we think we invoke the Law of Mind in Action and automatically receive a result, and since it is in the mind that we decide to do something, then *the Very Process of Deciding Causes Something to Happen.*

When we *decide* to rebuild our mental outlook, something happens—something always takes place, even if only a slight shifting of our mental awareness—and we find ourselves beginning to set into motion a new series of thoughts relative to the decision which we made.

But first the decision.

Some people say that they cannot make a decision—that it is impossible for them to decide *anything.* This is not true. We *all* have the power to make decisions and follow them through by our actions. We have the freedom and liberty, and we have the *ability* to use that freedom and liberty to set into motion a new series of thoughts and events, actions and reactions.

Through the use of the Law of Eradication, we can reject any and all thoughts, ideas, beliefs, things, and events from our awareness and reverse them mentally by correcting our outlook. *But We Must First Decide that We Can and Will Change Our Lives.*

LET'S NOT AFFIRM A LIE!

When we feel or affirm that we are *not* able to make a decision, *We Are Actually Affirming a Lack of Faith in God (the ability to use the Intelligence Within)*. The only way we will ever be able to make decisions enabling us to see, experience, and enjoy a new outlook is by learning to relax and putting a stop to our own mental resistance. Know with feeling:

> *I Am Intelligent, Therefore I Can Use That Intelligence to Change My Life.*

Realizing this, we must and will realize our ability to make a decision. Any time we come to a problem about which we find it hard to make a decision, *we can use this statement to clear out minds of all doubts.* Once that state of mind is achieved in which we have pushed away all doubt that would limit the recognition of our intelligence, we shall be ready to face the problem at hand. We shall be ready to *act!* We shall be able to think more clearly with the conviction of *knowing* that we can and will find an answer to any problem.

RELAXATION THE KEY

So the very first thing we must do is to clear our minds of any doubt or lack of confidence in our ability to use the

Intelligence that is in all of us. *It is through Relaxation that Our Subconscious Minds Will Attain the Rhythm and Harmony Which Will Make It Possible to Think Clearly and "Tune In" to the Universal Intelligence.* That's what we *really* mean by turning our will and life over to God as honestly as we know how, asking for guidance.

We simply relax. We become "still" in order to "know."

God (Universal Intelligence—Creative Energy) is reached through the subconscious mind. And *that* is reached only in a spirit and sense of *calm.* So the "answer" is "there," and often our conscious mind is *almost* aware of it. But the *mental resistance* makes us "blind" to its answer.

Any time we feel we cannot solve a problem or cannot make a decision, we must reverse our thinking and realize that *we are intelligent,* and so can use that Intelligence to change our lives. We must depend on the God-Power within—the "still, small voice" of Intelligence that is always there, ready to be listened to, if we will only take time to listen.

It begins with a decision and then moves into action—a thought in the mind and then a physical reaction, followed by action. Once we make a decision to change out life, we shall automatically be setting into motion those processes that in turn will begin to change our life *automatically.*

THE POWER OF PURE *KNOWING*

Once a decision is made, we must have the inner KNOW-ING that *something is going to take place!* Without that inner KNOWING, we are only fooling ourselves and merely mouthing our desires.

It is necessary to KNOW that something is going to take place, that something is going to *happen*. We have to KNOW that what we speak is exactly what we are thinking deep down in the subconscious. We must KNOW that we are not just mouthing our desires, but stating convictions. *We Must Be Convinced Something Is Going to Happen, and We Must Have a Mental Expectancy of What Will Take Place.*

Without expectancy, we are not really speaking our word with *conviction*. Only *conviction* will be expecting something to take place. And without KNOWING, we do not have the expectancy. When we are convinced of something, with a complete KNOWING, then we *automatically* have an expectancy of something about to take place.

THE JOY OF EXPECTANCY

Children approach a birthday or Christmas with the *expectancy* of receiving toys and gifts. They KNOW this will happen; they are convinced. And because they are convinced and KNOW they will receive toys and gifts, they have that excited *expectancy*.

The mind attracts what it really loves, fears, or expects. A successful young business executive once said, "I have found that it pays to have a high expectancy of good." Too many expect the worst. Perhaps things do look bleak once in a while; but why *expect* the worst or that they will get bleaker? Why not expect the sun to break through? Why not expect the best to happen? There is something magnetic about the way one thinks.

Through *expectancy*, we are awaiting something constructive; we are aware that **Something Good Is Going to Take Place, and Therefore We Are Looking for It to Take Place.**

But the person who is not expecting something constructive to take place *will not even see it when it does:* "That's not good; it only *looks* good . . . I'm not fooled!" *But he is!*

STEPPING UP TO ACCEPTANCE

Through *expectancy*, we are ready to *accept*. Without expecting something to take place, we shall not be ready to accept it when it does.

It Is Only through Acceptance that We Shall Be Able to Change Our Lives.

If we are not willing to recognize and *accept* the new for the old, then we shall not change. We must be ready and willing to accept our new heritage, our dominion over our lives, and identify ourselves with that infinite Source of all things—God (Intelligence). It is only thus that we shall ever be able to change our lives.

Once we make a decision, we must be ready for the outcome and the results of that decision. We must have some expectancy of what is about to come—automatically—as a result. And then, when the result does come, we must be able to recognize it for what it is *and accept it.*

THE "BIG THREE"

Without any one of these three—Decision, Expectancy, and Acceptance—we shall not achieve the first step in rebuilding our lives. We shall not achieve our happiness the scientific way, using the Power Within. *We Must Decide, Expect, and Accept*—the three powers to building a new life.

We do this by simply recognizing that there is *always* at the center of our being a place of peace, harmony, love, and intelligence. "God enters by a private door into each individual," said Ralph Waldo Emerson. It is *within us* and *up to us* to *accept.* Are we willing to continue to experience the results of our negative thoughts? *Or do we want to change our lives?*

If we want a new living experience that includes *only* happiness, love, and contentment, *we must (1) Decide to Change, (2) Expect Something to Happen as a Result, and (3) Be Ready to Recognize and Accept It When It Does Happen.* We *must* be looking for and recognizing everything that is harmonious, loving, intelligent, and giving. if we begin looking at things *positively*, that mental attitude will begin to express through us and, as a result, start projecting back.

For as we give, we receive.

SUMMING UP

⌇ We must recognize our Inner Intelligence (conscious union with God), acknowledging our ability to change our lives by simply changing our *awareness* and using our *mental* eyes and ears.

⌇ We must see and hear only those things that are in harmony with our new outlook—only those things that are positive and loving.

⌇ We must use the Law of Eradication to reject all impressions and expressions that are not a part of the world and experience we wish to become a part of. This means learning to see, hear, and experience *selectively.*

⌇ We must accept the happy result of all this.

It can be done. But it is up to *us* to decide, expect, and accept in *Now the Time!*

CHAPTER 11

HOW TO MATERIALIZE
YOUR WORD

*When we use our creative imagination in
strong faith, it will create for us, out of the
One Substance, whatever we have created in
thought. In this way man becomes a Co-
Creator with God.*

—Ernest Holmes

As WE SPEAK our word, something happens in the world around us, be it a material effect or only an emotional response. We cannot escape this.

But as we learn to consciously control our thoughts, only those effects that we desire will take place.

It is as simple as that.

THE SCIENTIFIC WAY TO CHANGE YOUR LIFE

Yet it would still seem almost too simple, too easy! But on examination of any truth, we see how simple it really is. The basic Truth is simple, but the *understanding* of it is complex.

Science explains that all matter breaks down to energy. What is energy? *Force.* What is force? The "invisible":

> *The worlds were framed . . . so that things which are seen were not made of things which do appear.* *

—the basic material of the Universe. And what directs *that* force? What *causes* it? The "Unknown"—that which we call God. The ultimate force, *Mind.* The creative force of the Universe, of God: *Intelligence.*

Take the nuclear reaction: a simple, natural principle, taking place all the time in the Universe around us—in the sun, in the stars—the coming together of two radioactive elements. They touch; and then the automatic reaction takes place. A simple contact of two atoms— *and a chain reaction is the result!*

---

* Hebrews 11:3

Thus the *concept* and the *event* are natural and simple. But it is the *controlling* and *directing* of this concept and its resultant energy that is difficult and time-consuming.

It is the same way with the principles of the Mind. It is the same way with learning to "materialize" our word. It takes time. It takes practice. It takes work. No matter how we use the Creative Process, *There Isn't a Thing We Can Do That Will Limit, Hinder, Tire, or Confuse It.*

BUT WE CAN MISDIRECT IT!

Nuclear power can be misdirected in the form of a destructive weapon instead of the powering of huge modern cities.

Mind can be misdirected, affecting our lives adversely; or it can be properly used to change our living experience into the happy, joyous expression of Love and Harmony that it is our right, freedom, and liberty to have.

The Universe is what it is because it follows certain mathematical laws that give it order and rhythm. It will go forth being what it is, evolving under the law of its own evolution. We are a part of the Universe and thereby follow the same laws of Creation. As the Universe is in an ever-changing growth, so are we. As the Universe works on an orderly pattern of action, so do we.

The Law cannot be changed, but we can use it for our own good. Just as the law of nuclear power can be used for our good when directed correctly, so the Law of Mind can be used for our good when used *scientifically.*

GOING WITH THE FLOW?

It's up to us to decide whether we are going to flow in the same inherently positive direction as the Law of Mind—*or go against it.* In the latter case, we are like a canoe trying to move upstream against overpowering currents—*but without paddles.*

It can't be done! And it will only waste energy!

Instead, if we will turn the canoe around and let the current's energy carry us along, relaxing and enjoying the free, effortless ride, we'll have time to look about us and take in the surrounding beauty.

By using the comparable energy within us in the same way, we can direct it toward useful, creative actions and emotional expressions. In any case, *We Must Either Fight It or Cooperate with It.*

FIRST: RELAX!

Yes, *RELAX!* Take it easy! Be Still! Listen! Part of the fight we put up against the stream of Mind in Action is by continuing to maintain our own personal opinions and human limitations—which are the cause of our problems.

But the knowledge we need is *within ourselves!* We don't have to fight, struggle, and run around chasing our own mental tails. The decision each one of us must make before we go one step further is: *Will it be upstream or downstream?* Wasted effort and energy—or that free ride?

Once we are in harmony with the Universal throb and pulse of God (all things in the Universe), then we will be ready to use our minds to direct and channel the power within, which will create a *chain reaction,* yielding a world

140

of new experiences. It is in this harmonious mental state that we project our word effectively.

Now we must KNOW that the word we speak or think is an outlet for the Universal Power. Our word caused something to happen. The Creative Power does and always will act upon the word that is spoken with conviction—not "mouthed," but believed in—KNOWN! Therefore whenever our conscious thinking begins entertaining doubts, we must relax and repeat this truth over and over until we have dropped from our awareness all resistance:

I AM IN THE MIDST OF
A LIMITLESS MEDIUM OF MIND.

We must realize that what is able to create must always create only on those principles that follow the laws of creation—or it would not be able to create. Any thing, action, or being that is creative, is creative only as long as it uses the laws of creation; otherwise creation would be impossible. This simply means that anything that is creative is using certain universal principles that are uniform with all things creative.

"MY WORD SHALL NOT RETURN TO ME VOID"

Our thoughts cause an effect. In doing this, they are, again, using certain basic principles that are creative. They automatically create an effect *as a result of their conviction. Thoughts Have Energy and Project Themselves into a Field That Responds to That Energy.*

Once we realize this truth *intellectually,* we will be ready to use it *effectively.* We shall be using it whether we are conscious of it or not. The whole idea is to learn to use the truth effectively, in the way we want, to get the desired effect.

"So shall my word be that goeth forth our of my mouth; it shall not return unto me void, but it shall accomplish that which I please," is the way the prophet Isaiah said it in the 7th century B.C.*

We never utter a word unless thinking of it first, either consciously or subconsciously. This is why our spoken words have power—not because *they themselves* have any power, but because they are thought of in the mind and are the result of that thought expressing itself through words.

For this same reason, if we begin consciously to redirect our words, to express only those qualities we wish to become part of our world, our experience, and our expression, then it follows that our minds will be compelled to think differently. *Once a decision has been made in the mind to become and do and express differently, we will automatically begin the changing process.*

PUT FEET ON THE DECISION

It is not enough just to make the decision. It must be followed with conscious and continued action and effort.

We can establish the same order within ourselves that is in the world around us when we think in larger terms

---

* Isaiah 55:11

and when we love with a love that includes all. We cannot express in a limited way. We cannot evolve from a limited viewpoint. We must not put obstacles in the way of our growth or expression. We must learn to become the thing that we wish to become by conscious effort.

This is done by redirecting our thought and energies in a harmonious way; by relaxing and letting the Mind current move us along,—taking the free ride; by the everyday effort of correcting our negative reactions to the world around us and reversing them so that we only see the positive.

We don't think in terms of "get me" or "give me" and threaten that "if you don't, I'll take [x] away." That is not what we mean. Accumulating, buying, storing, hoarding is not reaching out—but is holding back.

The thing we must work for is free circulation of that creative energy within us. If a block is put up against it, we don't stop its flow—we cannot do that—but we cause it to bypass us. If we do not love, we are not loved. If we do not express, we are not given any expression.

Our job is to become and express creatively as part of the world around us. If we put a resistance up against the flow, we are expending energy uselessly. Only when we begin relaxing with the flow do we use the creative energy within us in an effective way.

As we start moving with, instead of against, the Universal Rhythm, we find that our word *does* have power and that we can bring happiness and joy to the world around us. *As we love, we are loved. As we give, we receive.*

CIRCULATING GOOD

This is not giving with the mere idea of receiving as much as we can in return. It is giving in order that the flow can be continuous and circling. Then, as we receive, we give with the same degree, letting it pour out from us. It circles back, for it must. That is a very basic principle of the Universe. That which goes out far enough will circle back. Physics says as much.

But it is absurd to believe that this Law of Giving and Receiving should hold only on a physical level. The physical is an outgrowth of Mind. In the Mind it is thought; and as a result, it takes form by means of the Creative Power of the Universe and of all there is—God.

There is a pattern that all things follow, whether they are of the Mind or the material. Nothing comes out of nothing. Energy only changes form and goes on changing form again and again. As we project our thought into the Creative Force that responds to it, we are releasing a "charge" that will cause movement in a field of energy, which, in turn, causes movement within the physical.

Once a "charge" of mental energy—a thought—is projected, it must—and will—go somewhere and do something and become something. The "charge" will make or impress form in the physical, because that is its very nature. *Thoughts Are Things*—cause and effect.

THE DYNAMISM OF THOUGHTS

We don't hold thoughts; we *project* them. Each thought takes form and outwardly projects itself. We cannot stop thoughts from "escaping" us. They move and take form.

They Flow Outward and Have an Effect on Any Field or Thing or Item That They Touch.

Dropping a pebble into a pool of still water affects *all* the water. If we drop another, it will have its own effect. And as a third and fourth are dropped, they cause more and more rippling, all of which have effects on the rest.

Thoughts drop like pebbles into a pool of energy and cause their own ripples, each acting on the other, until a complex of actions and interactions has taken place. *If all the thoughts are of the same type, they will have a tendency to cause a pulsation within this pool that will work like a tidal wave.* If they are all *destructive,* they will combine to form destructive effects. If they are all *constructive,* they will cause overwhelmingly constructive effects.

If we have been thinking negatively but change to thinking positively, we shall be starting the neutralization of the negative waves, and finally we shall clear the darkness away, and only the light of Love will shine through. This is why it takes time—why we must work at it.

As a chemist knows, it is necessary to add an equal amount of one chemical to its opposite in order to neutralize it—then a little more of the chemical to change the solution from one kind to another—until negative becomes positive.

If it is dark and we wish to completely light the room, a simple candle will not do too well. It will cut down the darkness a little, but it will not light the whole room. Before darkness can be dispersed, we have to light *enough* candles to illuminate the *whole* room.

Twilight is not what we are after. We want a noonday sun to shine through our lives and experiences. We want a noonday sun shining through a clear sky, not one that is clouded or foggy with mists. In order to get the light of understanding and happiness expressing in our every thought, we must clear all the mists of misunderstanding and darkness away from our awareness.

We must move from dark to light. From negative to positive. From hate to Love. From night to day. And no grays. No in between.

IT ALL BEGINS—AND ENDS—WITH MIND

Power begins and ends in the actions of the mind. We must start at the mind and then expand from there. As nuclear energy is released when two elements are placed together, we can place our thinking in harmony with the Universal Rhythm and cause an energy explosion within our lives that will transform our experiences.

We have to start consciously and train our thinking until the subconscious responds and begins to think effectively. *We Must Project the Thoughts and Ideas and Energy Patterns That We Wish to Experience.*

By first using the Law of Eradication to erase all negative concepts and convictions from our minds, thoughts, and lives, and then by expressing through the Law of Circulation, we shall discover the surprising "secret" of God and Life.

As we learn Healing Prayer—*which is simply healing our thinking*—and then learn to express creatively, we shall find that all things will come unto us, and the necessity of conscious prayer will be eliminated from our lives, because each thought will be an effective prayer in *Now the Time!*

CHAPTER 12

YES, *NOW* THE TIME!

Now it is high time to awake out of sleep.

—Romans 13:11

NOT THE END. Not the end, but the beginning of a new, more fulfilling life. The conclusion of the old and the birth of the new, built on strong principles and strong convictions—Faith and KNOWING.

What this book has to say is really very simple: *Use Mind to Selectively See, Hear, Taste, Smell, Feel Remember, and Know—the Right, the Liberty, and the Freedom to Live the Life We Want to Live.*

But it is not the simplicity that we are after; rather, it is being able to understand the All as a simple idea and then working from this basic Truth in order to attract all things to us.

It is not easy to change. It is not easy to build a new life out of the rubble and shambles of the old. We never said it would be easy. If it were easy, the writing of this work or any other work of its kind would not be necessary, for we would all be practicing the principles that it has tried to explain.

By using the Law of Eradication, we erase from our experiences all those things we do not wish to be our reality.

By using the Law of Circulation, we accept what God has offered us and we give with the same spirit of givingness.

For as we give, we receive.

SCIENCE OF MIND, SCIENCE OF LIFE

This is the time of science. We need not accept anything that does not follow natural laws. Science and religion are not opposites. They are equally intelligent attempts to understand the unknown. "Those who speak of the incompatibility of science and religion either make science say that which it never said or make religion teach that which it never taught" (Pius XI).

But "God only helps those who help themselves." We are all given a chance in life, one time or another, to face up to the test of our faith: we either sink or swim.

"The Kingdom of God is within." It is within us to change our lives. It is within us to correct our inner KNOWING to accept only those things that will enrich our lives:

Love for hate.

Youthfulness for old age.

There is no such thing as time, only the ever-present *now*. *Now* we can change our lives. Not yesterday. Not tomorrow.

We Begin Now!

31 PRAYER-MEDITATIONS
FOR A MONTH'S WORTH OF *NOW!*

THE FOLLOWING Spiritual Mind-Stretching exercises (Meditations) are arranged so as to build our awareness, understanding, and ability to KNOW—each day. It is a step-by-step ascent to the paradise above and beyond our present experience.

As we repeat each of these meditations, KNOWING that they are the Truth of our being, we will be climbing upwards to the fulfillment of the happiness which is ours for the asking.

These are not magic words. They are not secret formulas for successful living. They are only words. It is up to *us* to KNOW their Truth, not just to mouth them. Without our KNOWING, they will have no effect on our lives.

Yet, if we have not attained that evolvement which is necessary to get the answer to all our prayers each and every time, it is not only foolish but dangerous to just say our word and let it go at that. If an ailment affects our lives and we have not evolved to that state of being which will automatically remove this error from our experience, then it is right and correct to go to someone who can scientifically help us—a physician, or a person of greater understanding—to advise us of the right action to take.

What follows, then, is not only meditations but mental experiences for the developing of our mental muscles and awareness so that we can use the art of selective seeing.

Understand their meaning.

Believe what they say.

KNOW THEM!

MEDITATION 1

"The reason for the Law is the Law" (Sir Walter Scott).

I accept the intuition of God that reveals to me my heritage. I now clear my thoughts of all doubts, fears, or questions. I know that infinite intelligence guides me into my true expression of life. I know that all secrets for my health and peace of mind are now opened to me. I am in this awareness kin to all mankind. The divine love of God sets me on the path of everlasting happiness.
And so it is.

MEDITATION 2

"It shall be done unto you as you believe." In the communion of prayer, that which we desire passes from the invisible to the visible. Dr. Ernest Holmes said, "I believe that my faith operates upon the Law of Mind, which automatically manifests in my experience according to that faith."

In the deep inner peace that comes from my complete acceptance of the living God, I release all fears, condemnation, resentment, and know that my life is filled with new strength, courage, and vision. I know that this is now in effect through me, and I accept this truth of my being.
And so it is.

MEDITATION 3

In reading from that old classic *Letters of the Scattered Brotherhood*, one will find this passage: "The inner wishes of your hearts are known. Resolve; marshal your will and your intent! Find your purpose and direction! Then will you be sustained and comforted and reminded of the Presence in this Holy Place." The Holy Place is within the recesses of our own Being, for we each individualize the Universe Itself according to our own perception.

Our Father, in confidence I recognize within me the only activity and presence—that of God. This life is mine, this strength is mine. Every day in the depth of my inner thought I recognize this Presence. I grow and expand in an increased awareness of my spiritual conjunction, more each day than the day before.
And so it is.

MEDITATION 4

Thomas Carlyle, thinking of his home, said: "Thank Heaven, I know and have known what it is to be a son and love a father—as Spirit can love Spirit. God gives me to live to my Father's honor and His." As we individually embrace the idea of the Love of God, KNOWING that God is ever present in our activity and thought, we ourselves are embodying the Truth as stated—"as Spirit can love Spirit." In this way the Grace of God becomes instantly revealed. The Father-Son relationship holds new promise, and its manifestation in our activities becomes complete fulfillment.

I accept no problem too difficult for the Father Within to solve. I KNOW that all things are possible through Him. I relax and turn everything over to God—my health, my supply, my safety, and my love. The wisdom of the living Spirit now guides and directs me in all my affairs. And so it is.

MEDITATION 5

"I will rejoice that from all tormenting we can retreat always upon the Invisible Heart, upon the Celestial Love, and that not to be compensated, but to receive power to make all things new" (Ralph Waldo Emerson).

At this moment, I give thanks that all my needs are fulfilled. KNOWING this, I remove every destructive memory, fear, or doubt of the past, and KNOW that confidence and certainty are present in all decisions. In all things I now practice what I believe, for there is only the perfect right action of God expressing in my thinking, feeling, and experiencing.
And so it is.

MEDITATION 6

"Ignorance of the law excuses no man; not that all men know the law, but because it is an excuse every man will plead, and no man can tell how to confute him" (John Selden). We KNOW, and Jesus did, that there is a definite law of God that operates through us and reacts to our thoughts. A confession that we don't know the law is no valid excuse. The law of action and reaction is as old as creation—it is immutable and accordingly acts whether we wish to acknowledge it or not. "Love rules through Law"—the Love of God, incarnate within each one, operates in our life and activities as we give it out freely and as we accept its existence.

I now am secure and poised in the acceptance of the divine Presence expressing through me. I recognize that the law of Spirit shall respond to my every idea and thought. I know that my every thought is one of abundance, wholeness, and harmonious activity. I am a complete expression of God, therefore my work, relations, activities, home, and church life respond through the law of Mind to this infinite truth.
And so it is.

MEDITATION 7

"To have ideas is to gather flowers; to think is to weave them into garlands" (Madame Swetchine, 16th-century Russian mystic). As we free our minds and hearts from mental attitudes unlike God—such as anger, resentment, fear, insecurity, and turmoil—the ideas of the Universe flow through us individually. The feeling is akin to that of the ecstasy experienced when gathering fresh-cut pine boughs or flowers from our garden, seemingly dipped in sunlight. As we focus our attention with a willing self-discipline, the ideas pour into visible form that is indeed a weaving of garlands.

I KNOW that what I think about must become so. I KNOW that I must attract to me that upon which I think. I therefore dwell only upon the thought of God expressing through me in my every activity. Today I am grateful for the flow of divine ideas into my every experience. I am young in spirit, and my energy, youth, and optimism are continuously renewed.
And so it is.

MEDITATION 8

The first Epistle General of John, which was written approximately 90 A.D. and dedicated to the "11th Commandment" of love, says in the third chapter, second verse: "Beloved, NOW are we the Sons of God." We are all Sons of God, and all of us partake of the divine Nature. God's Love is complete within each one of us. As we accept the NOW and not the hereafter, the Sonship of Freedom gives birth to the awareness that "Today is the day of complete salvation."

I KNOW that God is always where I am. I KNOW that today I receive God everywhere. I KNOW that this acceptance now dissolves all fear, lack, or inadequacy. I see the Divine in every person or situation in my life. I am constantly expanding in an increased awareness of my sonship, for this is the way, the truth, and the life. And so it is.

MEDITATION 9

"The underlying cause of all weakness and unhappiness in man has always been, and still is, weak habit of thought" (Horace Fletcher). We must concentrate our attention in order to form the mold of what we desire. It is good to know that we have within us the right to use God's creativeness for greater expression and for peace that passes all understanding. As we daily reaffirm the recognition of Truth and Presence of Spirit, we prepare the way for constant happiness. Not sporadic happiness—caused by calling on God at a moment of stress—but all the time.

As I accept the divine truth of God, I am aware of a surging power and wisdom that emanate from within me and know no barrier. Recognizing that all things increase after their kind, I KNOW that I now express a faith that removes all doubt and lifts my understanding to the pinnacle of all understanding. Thus my oneness frees me from all but the confidence and expectancy of the richer, fuller life.
And so it is.

MEDITATION 10

"Perfect Truth is possible only with knowledge, and in knowledge, the whole essence of the thing operates on the soul and is joined essentially to it" (Spinoza). It has been said that "the Christ Spirit is the Spirit of Truth." With our knowledge and conviction of the Indwelling Presence of God—with our knowledge and conviction that Truth is God—our emotions, feelings, sensitivities respond with joy, peace, happiness, and an ever-abiding love of humankind. The Soul of man becomes the true reflection. This is the true Christ Awareness.

I KNOW that today all the wisdom of the living Spirit comes to my assistance. I NOW accept the harmonious relationship to my divine existence. I am aware, today, of my identity with the "Peace that passes all understanding." Today I dedicate my mind to the highest good, KNOWING the highest good is revealed to me. Today I eradicate from my thought anything unlike the Christos of my God self. Today I prepare for the birth of awareness. And so it is.

MEDITATION 11

"Whatever that be which thinks, understands, wills, and acts, it is something celestial and divine" (Cicero). Ernest Holmes says that true healing means *mind* healing. We strive to heal people's mentalities, knowing that to the degree we are successful, we can heal the body. Belief in duality makes us sick, but understanding of our oneness with God will heal us. This applies as well to all our issues and affairs.

I KNOW that the infinite Spirit is everywhere, therefore where I am, God is. I KNOW that this perfect realization frees me from all apprehension. I am aware of an inflow of constant health and well-being. My body and mind respond to this divine power. In this acceptance no external condition can bind me. I now radiate only thoughts that uplift, vitalize, and immerse me in the radiance of a whole "Temple of the Living God."
And so it is.

MEDITATION 12

In the 1600s there resided in France a philosopher and scientist named Blaise Pascal. His passing at the age of 39 made hardly a ripple at the time. However, this man, later renowned as a mathematician and philosopher, bequeathed a formula for future generations: "Imagination disposes of everything; it creates beauty, justice, and happiness, which are everything in this world."

As we utilize the divine Power of choice we can envision peace, nations living in harmony, and the world free from strife. As we vision, we receive our reward in a complete embodiment of universal accord.

At this moment I surrender myself completely to God. Right NOW I accept only the fulfillment in my life of God's truth, wisdom, and understanding. At this moment, I have complete trust in the sureness of divine unchanging perfect action. I have the certain faith to KNOW that I stand in the center of limitless opportunity. For I KNOW what where I am, God is.
And so it is.

MEDITATION 13

"Pray to God at the beginning of all thy works, that thou mayest bring them all to a good ending" (Xenophon). We, as wonderful human individuals, have the habit of praying or asking God to intercede only when we have immersed ourselves in disorder and confusion.

If we, by affirmative prayer, pray at the beginning of our projects or days KNOWING that the Indwelling God directs us, we accordingly choose the direction of abundance and right action.

I recognize my right to strength, courage, wholeness, abundance, and joy as my divine heritage. I KNOW that my ability to pray rests in this complete acceptance of fact. I KNOW that I am a part of all humankind and all life. I KNOW my every need is NOW fulfilled. I KNOW that God is where I am NOW. I am grateful for this communion of prayer. In it I renew my faith and thus I am "born again."
And so it is.

MEDITATION 14

There is an ancient Arabian proverb that clearly states the Law of Life: "He who has health has hope; and he who has hope, has everything." When our minds, hearts, and being are balanced with the rhythm of the Universe, and when we KNOW that we can turn to this within ourselves, then we reflect this recognition of Living Spirit in our bodies. When we do that, we have health. When we are healthy, we look forward with expectancy to the unfoldment of Life's riches and truth. We have everything.

I KNOW that I am a source of constant bubbling health and happiness, for this stems from the eternal spring of all life incarnated within me. I remember that, as St. Paul has told us, "God has given me no spirit of fear but only that of power, love, and a sound mind."
And so it is.

MEDITATION 15

"When you doubt, abstain" (Zoroaster). It has been said that if you doubt the wisdom of a choice of experience you are making—don't do it. The wisdom of the ages has led us to the techniques of Spiritual Mind Healing. When we have entered into communion in prayer, and doubt still, we have not fully accepted the idea of "God's Law" working. We have not released fears and turned the problem over to God. The answer is simple—abstain, but pray until the doubt is removed and the right action has revealed itself.

I NOW release to God all anxieties, doubts, and fears. I NOW accept the flow of divine confidence filling the recesses of my being. I KNOW that God is my only director and God is my only answer. I am completely identified with the realization that the truth of man is "perfect God, perfect Man, perfect Being."
And so it is.

MEDITATION 16

"Visible deeds do not increase the goodness of the inner life, whatever their number or dimension; they can never be worth much if the inward process is small or nonexistent, and they can never be of little worth if the inner process exists and is great" (Meister Eckhart).

As we within our own heart and minds unify with the unassailable Truth of God—recognition of Beauty, Kindness, Gratitude, Friendship, and Integrity—the outer is made whole. I recognize my affinity with all of nature.

I recognize and identify myself only with beauty, truth, and wisdom. I KNOW that I reflect the wholeness of the Divine in my body. I KNOW that I respond to God's Love from my family. I KNOW that I accept the respect of my associates as my divine heritage. I extend my every thought to graciously receive the gifts of the infinite Creator of us all: beauty, kindness, gratitude, friendship, and integrity.
And so it is.

MEDITATION 17

In 1695, Archbishop Francis Fénelon of France uttered a simple statement that offers to the world and to the individual the peace so earnestly sought after: "Speak, move, act in Peace, as if you were in prayer. In Truth, this *is* Prayer."

I NOW surrender all confusion, disorder, disharmony, and temper. My every thought and word is NOW identified with only order, harmony, and balanced emotions. I am revealing in my life, every instant, the calm of the divine Presence. I KNOW that I accept my relationship to the peace that passes all human understanding. I KNOW that God is everywhere. This peace of God is NOW reflecting in my home, in my dealings with others, and in my every expression.
And so it is.

MEDITATION 18

We hold on to old patterns and habits and anxieties for fear of losing an old "friend." When we accept that we are *losing nothing*—but are *eradicating the negative*—then we realize the Truth of our individual happiness. All men, women, children, objects, jobs, situations, and experiences proceed from one source, and that source is *God*. Let us today, as we accept this Truth, *Let go and let God*.

I KNOW that the wisdom of the Infinite Creator of us all guides, directs, and sustains me forevermore. I release, at this instant, all worries, doubts, and anxieties. I give no place in my life to any falseness or anything unlike the truth of my nature. This truth is calmness, confidence, enthusiasm, and the never-ending flow of divine Principle through me and my affairs. Believing in the right action of Spirit, I NOW let go and let God. And so it is.

MEDITATION 19

"As soon as a man turneth himself in spirit, and with his whole heart and mind entereth into the mind of God which is above time, all that he hath ever lost is restored in a moment" *(Theologia Germanica)*. If the Universe is controlled by Intelligence, *and it is*, and if intelligence is an action of Mind, *and it is*, then God must be Mind; and accordingly, the laws of God must be mental laws. Jesus said, "Come unto me all ye who travail and are heavy laden and I will refresh you."

I accept at this moment that the health, mental poise, and peace in my life emanate from the divine Source Itself. Today I KNOW that truth releases all fear or doubt. I KNOW that everything that partakes of the nature of the divine Reality I accept as my own.
And so it is.

MEDITATION 20

Mark Twain tells a quaint story of the man who spent years in prison, only to walk out one morning when he discovered the doors had never been locked. We, as individuals, have within us the freedom of the Universe. Because of its very nature, we bind ourselves with freedom itself. Now, this minute, *open the door—it is unlocked*. Our problem need not be.

We can choose our own pathways.

I am free from all resentment and self-pity. I am free from mistakes and their effects on me. The only law that I use in my life is the law of God, which operates through me. I KNOW that I am free to accept the goals of my life: harmony, poise, balance, health, and happiness. In this acceptance, I am sustained and directed forever. And so it is.

MEDITATION 21

"Faultily faultless, splendidly null, dead perfection, no more" (Alfred, Lord Tennyson). We forget that sometimes our healing of mind or body is prevented because we have escaped to an image of form perfect in outline but with no sincere conviction or feeling that God is every cell in our bodies.

I give thanks that I can feel the divine Love abound, within and throughout my entire being. I see in others only that which is good. I hear only that which speaks well of another. I speak only a word that blesses. I am sure and certain of the law of God that guides my every footstep. And so it is.

MEDITATION 22

"Look with wonder at that which is before you" (St. Clement of Alexandria). Our hearts and minds should always be filled with the beauty of all Creation. The expectancy of the continual unfolding of Nature's wonders removes all clouds of doubt or discordance from our minds if we must look and see.

I NOW dispel all thought of sorrow, for as I open my heart and mind to the never-ending flow of the divine joy in my life, I can recognize nothing else. I KNOW that revitalization which quickens my senses and directs me individually in an unceasing pathway of God's delight. And so it is.

MEDITATION 23

Ralph Waldo Emerson, in his essay on Spiritual Law, gives this account of the Law of Attraction: "Everything the individual sees without him, corresponds to his state of mind."

We draw to us, in our lives, events of happiness when we are happy. When we feel despair, we seem to encounter it at every turn. When we feel successful, everything we touch is a success. When we feel healthy and whole, we surround our family and life with health and wholeness. When we love another, we have many who love us. It is only as we feel and see the Perfect joy and happiness of the Indwelling God that it is expressed in our lives.

I release all mental attitudes that could disturb my body, family life, relationships, or business activities. I KNOW that every thought activates only the experiences of well-being. I recognize in others the qualities I seem to express. I KNOW that each new day I am a part of the universal Heart and Mind. I KNOW that my limitless self expands each day to the greater, fuller realization of divine kinship. I am, at this moment, drawn to that which fulfills my life to the utmost degree.
And so it is.

MEDITATION 24

"How blind men are to Heaven's gifts" (Lucan). The abundance of life, peace, and security that we all desire surrounds us constantly. As we day by day realize the impossibility of God containing any counterpart of limitation, we increase our abundance. Responding to the karmic Law of Cause and Effect, we are at the sum total of our thoughts and experiences. When we accept limitation as a personally imposed mental attitude, then we have taken the first step to abundance materially, spiritually, and physically.

I identify myself NOW with the infinite Source of all supply. I KNOW that I am led, directed, and sustained by God. I release any idea that God is punishing or imposing limitation upon my being or affairs. I am expanding, daily, in wisdom, understanding, and acceptance of God's expression through me as an individual. These words NOW open all doors for my ever-increasing abundance. I am divinely prospered in all ways of life.
And so it is.

MEDITATION 25

In 1650 Richard Baxter, an English divinity student, said: "We reach perfection not by copying, but by constantly and steadily working out the life which is common to all, according to the Character which God has given us. The more perfect the sight is, the more delightful the beautiful object." We are prone to see only the effects, such as hatred, lack, illness, or anxiety, forgetting that the other individual has the same God Nature that we have. As we realize it, our sight becomes clearer and the other person becomes in our sight what we are.

As a complete expression of God, I NOW recognize the divine Nature within everyone that I meet, speak to, or KNOW. I realize that from deep within I radiate the peace, harmony, and love of my divine self. I surrender to this perfect understanding and KNOW that this power is directing me on the path of perfect self-expression. And so it is.

MEDITATION 26

When we stop questing for *time* and accept the Eternal NOW—then success is ours. Too often we, by our own thinking, delay the success of our lives. At all times we either attract or repel our success. This success, reflected in our activities, is determined by the strength of our conviction, as spoken by the apostle Paul, that "NOW is the appointed time."

As I NOW recognize that I am a creation of God, I KNOW that there can be no failures or limitations in my activities. I KNOW that my success is that of the Divine Itself and that there can be no failures or limitations in my activities. I KNOW that my success is that of the Divine Itself and that today I will not be engulfed by worry, fear, or anxiety. I bless my business—my personal career—my customers—my associates. I do this in the knowledge, sure and certain, that the wisdom of the living Spirit directs my affairs.
And so it is.

MEDITATION 27

G. K. Chesterton, an early 20th-century essayist, said: "The moment you step into the world of facts, you step into the world of limits. You can free things from alien or accidental laws, but not from the laws of their nature." We, as individuals, have a tendency to prevent our good from manifesting, due to our belief that God is separated from us. We are prone to be governed by figures as a statistician might see them. This limits our concept. We can know the Truth that the Law of God is present everywhere. We can step aside from the figures but not from God. *Herein lies our freedom.*

I KNOW that my every idea is God-directed. I express the one Life Principle, which is God. I radiate, in every way, peace, right action, and divine Law. KNOWING that there is only one law of Mind, I speak and think only thoughts of God's love. I KNOW that the one fundamental law fills my every experience with peace, security, and enthusiasm.
And so it is.

MEDITATION 28

"Time, whose tooth gnaws away everything else, is powerless against Truth" (Thomas Henry Huxley). The corrosions of previous experiences, fancied wrongdoings, and hurts to others, have a tendency to age us chronologically. However, for those accepting the timeless Truth of the ever-living Spirit acting in their lives, this process is neutralized. "The Truth shall set you free."

I NOW stand at the threshold of a period of greater creativity in my life. I open wide my heart, mind, and being to an inflow of spiritual enthusiasm. I discard all unhappy thoughts of the past. I forgive all wrongs, real or imaginary. I KNOW that each day's experiences express happiness, prosperity, and divine Guidance. I give thanks for the indwelling God reflected in my every situation and activity.
And so it is.

MEDITATION 29

Ralph Waldo Trine, philosopher and author on *In Tune with the Infinite,* regarded as one of the outstanding forerunners of New Thought concepts, has said: "Put all wishes aside save the one desire to know Truth. Couple with this, one demand: the fully consecrated determination to follow what is distinctly perceived as Truth, immediately it is revealed." The expression of the mystic personality requires a conscious effort 24 hours a day. The paramount desire must be to KNOW the Truth; and when the Truth becomes apparent, we must learn to recognize it and not say, "This couldn't be God!" but instead feel and say that "This too is of the Divine." And as we watch, we see.

I realize that today is a new day. I KNOW that I express the one Life Principle, which is God. I radiate the peace, harmony, and love of my divine self. I speak and think only thoughts of good to others and to myself. I KNOW that my heart and mind reflect only appreciation of the opportunities presented to me in my life. I KNOW that this is the law of God in action forever in my experience. I KNOW I am NOW a creative expression of God, and that I will always be so. And as I speak my word . . . so it is.

MEDITATION 30*

Faith is more than an objective statement. We do not have perfect faith while any subjective contradictions deny the affirmation of our lips.

Today I have faith that my word shall not return unto me void. Today I surrender myself completely to this faith, for I know that there is a creative Spirit which gives substance to this faith and which will provide the evidence of this substance in actual fact. I expect, then, to meet my good, and I rejoice in the anticipation of this good. I know that my faith operates through an immutable Law and that there is no possibility whatsoever of its failing.

* From Ernest Holmes, *14 Mental Treatments.*

MEDITATION 31*

Every man is "dear to the heart of God." We should all develop an increasing consciousness that we are protected and guided in everything we do, say, or think.

Today I know that the Spirit goes before me, making plain my way. I feel that everything I do shall be prospered and I fully accept that I am in partnership with the Infinite. It is my desire that only good shall go from me, therefore I have a right to expect that only good shall return to me. I live under the government of Good and am guided by the Spirit of God. This I affirm; this I accept.

---

* From Ernest Holmes, *14 Mental Treatments.*